Junk Drawer
ALGEBRA

50 AWESOME ACTIVITIES | That Don't Cost a Thing

T0001816

BOBBY MERCER

CHICAGO REVIEW PRESS

Published by Chicago Review Press Incorporated
814 North Franklin Street
Chicago, Illinois 60610
ISBN 978-1-64160-098-9

Library of Congress Cataloging-in-Publication Data
Names: Mercer, Bobby, 1961- author.
Title: Junk drawer algebra : 50 awesome activities that don't cost a thing /
    Bobby Mercer.
Description: Chicago, Illinois : Chicago Review Press Incorporated, [2019] |
    Audience: Age 9-12. | Audience: Grade 4 to 6. | Includes bibliographical
    references.
Identifiers: LCCN 2019014854 (print) | LCCN 2019017588 (ebook) | ISBN
    9781641600996 (adobe pdf) | ISBN 9781641601016 (epub) | ISBN 9781641601009
    (kindle) | ISBN 9781641600989 (trade paper)
Subjects: LCSH: Algebra—Juvenile literature.
Classification: LCC QA141 (ebook) | LCC QA141 .M47 2019 (print) | DDC
    512.9—dc23
LC record available at https://lccn.loc.gov/2019014854

Cover design: Andrew Brozyna
Interior design: Jonathan Hahn
Interior photos: Bobby Mercer

Printed in the United States of America
5 4 3 2 1

To teachers everywhere, continue to challenge the future generations

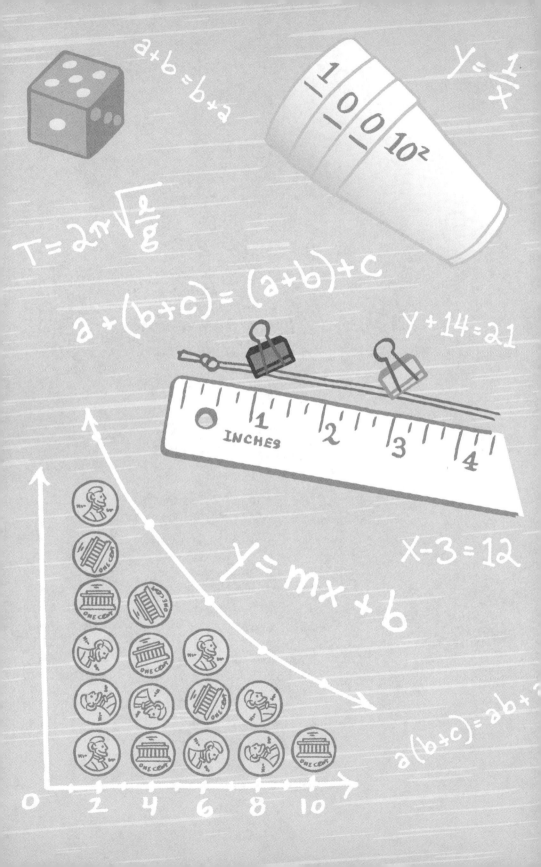

Contents

3 Algebra Labs   93

Acknowledgments

Books don't happen without great people helping along the way. Thanks to Kathy Green, the best agent in the business. Thanks to Jerome Pohlen and the gifted people at Chicago Review Press for having the courage to publish a math book for everybody.

Thanks to the wonderful people I work with; their thoughts, ideas, and encouragement mean the world to me. Shannon Haynes, Jennifer Allsbrook, Ethan Abbott, and Leslie Rhinehart have been invaluable as shoulders to lean on. To Brandon Schweitzer, Josh Hill, Michelle Travieso, and Aaron Greene, thanks for being supportive in all the right ways. As always, thanks to my wonderful better half, Michele, and my two partners in hands-on mayhem, Nicole and Jordan.

Introduction

This book will help you turn math lessons into a hands-on playground with everyday items. As a longtime science teacher, I've learned that many students benefit from a kinesthetic learning environment. Adding visual and hands-on components to math is essential for students to get the basics.

Math, like science, eventually reaches levels that can be skyscraper high. But at the bottom of a good skyscraper is a solid foundation, and all ability levels need that solid base. You also need excitement about the topic. If you excite a child early about math, you hook that child for life. Unlike science, math needs help to be hands on, and I hope *Junk Drawer Algebra* can add to that excitement. Some of these activities were used at my house to engage my daughters in math thinking.

The projects in this book all use everyday items that most people already have around their house. Many of these projects explore topics I teach in a science setting because math is the language of physics. All students benefit from a hands-on environment in virtually any arena. You learn to ride a bike by doing it. You should learn math by doing it. *Junk Drawer Algebra* is a great tool to help children "get" math.

One of my favorite sayings is "To teach them you have to reach them." A fun activity is a way to do that. Even if it just takes five minutes, it may pay you back as a teacher when your students are engaged. Math also could use a dose of creativity. Many of these activities are just fun, artistic ways to help learn math. Many non-math-oriented students love art, so use that to hook them. Maybe art and hands-on activities are what math needs. I personally have added many fun activities to the teaching of physics. Such activities grab the students and prepare them for more complex topics in advanced math classes.

Some of these activities demonstrate the usefulness of math. Students often ask their math teachers, "Why do we have to learn this?" Math is the language of science and engineering, but students often don't see the correlation. A few activities in this book might be as much science as math, but they do a tremendous job of showing the integration of the two subjects. Cross-curricular activities are a great idea in the school setting. They might be an even better idea for homeschooled students or for students who are just naturally curious.

To start things off, I have included how to make your own whiteboards for less money than buying prepared whiteboards. They can be used for many of the projects in this book.

Student Whiteboards

Make your own set of classroom whiteboards for under $20.

Adult supervision required

From the Junk Drawer:

- ☐ Sheet of white bathroom wall paneling (also called white tile boards, often sold at major hardware stores)
- ☐ Power saw
- ☐ Sandpaper (optional)

Step 1: Visit your local home improvement store and buy one (or two) sheets of white bathroom wall paneling. Many home improvement stores are set up to cut panels for you. If a sales assistant can't cut all the pieces for you, he or she may be willing to split it in half, which will make it easier to get the paneling home. Another option is to ask if the store has any broken panels. Oftentimes one corner of a panel is damaged and the store will sell it at a discount. Once you're home, cut the paneling into 12-inch-by-16-inch rectangles (making 24 whiteboards per sheet) or 12-inch-by-24-inch rectangles (16 whiteboards per sheet). The paneling can be cut with a normal power saw and blade. If you are a high school or middle school teacher and your school teaches carpentry or woodshop, the carpentry or shop teacher will likely be glad to cut the paneling if you ask. Once the panels are cut, you can use sandpaper to smooth any sharp edges.

The Math Behind It

Giving students individual whiteboards is a cheap and easy way to let them write, calculate, and fix mistakes easily using dry-erase markers. It also makes classroom monitoring of student learning easier because you can easily see each student's work. Plus, kids love drawing on them.

Giving whiteboards to my students might be the best thing I ever did in my teaching career. I created a set 20 years ago that I still use today, either individually or in pairs, at least twice a week. The dry-erase ink cleans easily with paper towels, though I now have a shoebox full of erasers for students to use.

You can buy whiteboards, but two boards from a store will cost you more than an entire panel of bathroom paneling. For homeschooling, buying a single board may be the way to go. Store-bought whiteboards have one advantage in that they usually have a metal backing that makes them magnetic and easy to mount on walls.

Math for the Ages

The boards are a hit with all ages. Since they're small and portable, they are great for car trips or for math or science practice.

1

Algebra Activities

M ath should be enjoyable, but at the same time, math should also teach you things you don't know. The patterns and quirks of math make it fun. Whether you are a parent, teacher, or a young learner yourself, adding a little fun to math is always a good thing. Enjoy these activities and smile. Math rocks!

Calculator Tricks

Here are several math tricks to practice using your calculator.

Algebra Concepts: Using a calculator, the **commutative property**

From the Junk Drawer:
☐ Calculator

Three-Six-Three Digits

Step 1 Pick any three-digit number and enter it twice into your calculator. For example, the number 345 would be entered as 345345.

Step 2: Divide the number by 7.

Step 3: Divide the number by 11.

Step 4: Divide the number by 13. What do you notice about the resulting number? Now try this for an extension: Start with the same six-digit number you had in Step 1, then do Steps 2, 3, and 4 in a new order—for example, Step 3, Step 4, and then Step 2. What number do you end up with? This is a great way to "read the mind" of a friend (or a student, if you are the teacher).

Three-Six-Three Digits, Part 2

Step 5: Pick any three-digit number. Multiply it by 7.

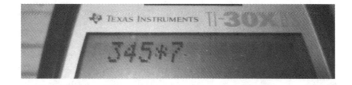

Step 6: Multiply the number by 11.

Step 7: Multiply the number by 13. What do you notice about the number? Now try this for an extension of Part 2: Start with the same three-digit number you had in Step 5, then multiply by 7, 11, and 13, in any order. What number do you end up with?

The Math Behind It

These calculator tricks demonstrate a few math quirks.

For the Three-Six-Three Digits trick, the secret is that $7 \times 11 \times 13$ is equal to 1,001. Any three-digit number multiplied by 1,001 would result in the same three-digit number written twice. Using division, you are simply dividing your six-digit number (made up of repeating three-digit numbers) by 1,001, so you get the first three digits of the six-digit number you started with.

Math for the Ages

This is great practice for using a calculator and a great way to show your ability to "read minds." This is great for teachers who have five minutes left at the end of class.

Candy Graphs

Use M&Ms to create **pie graphs**, **bar graphs**, and study **probability**.

Algebra Concepts: Probability, and graphing

From the Junk Drawer:

☐ Bag of M&Ms

☐ Clean, blank paper (or clean whiteboard)

☐ Clean, new straw (optional)

☐ Marker

Step 1: Separate a bag of M&Ms into the different colors. Do it on a clean, blank piece of paper or a clean whiteboard, so you can eat your equipment at the end of the activity.

Step 2: Carefully move the different colors into a pie graph. To keep the candy clean, use a clean, new straw to move them. Each color should represent a different wedge of the pie.

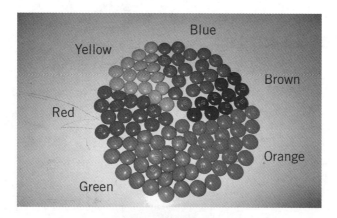

Step 3: Now create a bar graph using the different colors. Write the number
of pieces up the side axis and the different colors grouped together on the
bottom axis. Depending on the size bag you use, the total numbers for
each color will be different, but the distribution should be about the same.

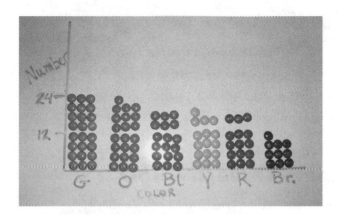

The Math Behind It

Pie graphs and bar graphs are two of the first graphs students learn about. Pie
graphs are perfect when you are trying to figure out the part of a whole. Any
size bag of M&Ms can be turned into an almost perfect circle. In the real
world, pie graphs are also usually accompanied by percentages, where the entire
pie represents 100 percent.

Bar graphs are also a way to visualize numbers. For this graph, each bar
represents a different color of M&M, but you could graph students' hair color,
eye color, birth month, and so on.

Probability is the possibility of getting a certain result divided by the number of chances. For the bag pictured, there were 24 green M&Ms and 104 total
candies. When you reach in a new bag, you should have a 24 out of 104 chance
of picking a green M&M. M&M data is an average and could vary from bag to
bag, but it should be roughly the same. Compare students' findings to information found online. Though the company that produces M&Ms no longer posts
statistical color data online, a lot of data exists on the Internet because people
do activities similar to this one. (The M&Ms website does say, however, that the
colors all have the same taste, no matter what your favorite color might be.)

In the study of algebra, graphs take center stage. These early graphs are helpful in giving students a starting point. Probability is usually taught as a separate subject in Algebra 2 but is easy to grasp with a good start early.

Math for the Ages

This is a fun way to introduce pie and bar graphs. It is also a great activity in a classroom, because groups can compare their data to other groups. For a class setting, the small fun-size bags may be the way to go. This activity could also be extended into probability for older students.

Coordinate Three in a Row

Practice **coordinates** with a friend in this fun game.

Algebra Concept: Coordinates (or **ordered pairs)**

From the Junk Drawer:

☐ Paper

☐ Pencil or marker

☐ 2 different-colored dice

☐ Several tokens of 2 different types (such as pennies and nickels, poker chips, etc.)

Step 1: Draw a 6-by-6 grid on a piece of paper.

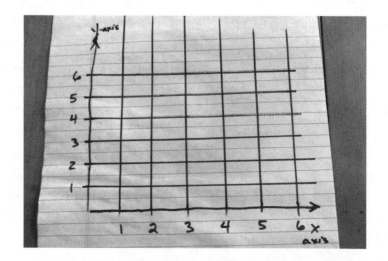

Step 2: Pick one color die to represent the *x*-coordinate and the other to represent the *y*-coordinate. If you don't have two different-colored dice, you could color on one with a permanent marker.

The youngest player goes first. Roll both dice. The player then places one of his or her markers at the ordered pair shown on the dice.

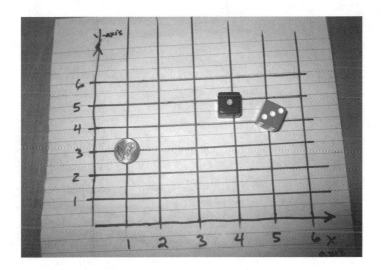

Step 3: The other player goes next. If the second player rolls an ordered pair that already has a marker on it, he or she must roll again. (Or, as an alternative, he or she could stack a new marker on the other player's marker.)

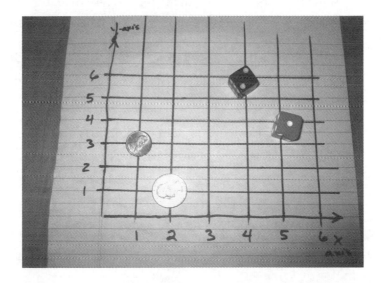

Step 4: Alternate rolling of the dice until one player gets three ordered pairs in a row, either vertically, horizontally, or diagonally. (In the example shown, the winner was circled to make it easier to see, but don't write on the grid—it can be reused.)

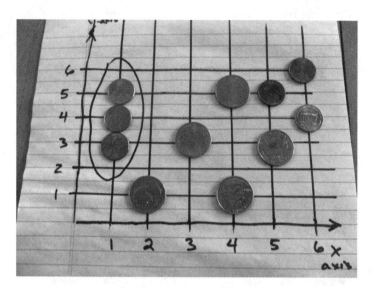

The Math Behind It

Coordinate systems are basic to the study of algebra. Ordered pairs are called coordinates by some teachers. They follow the form (x,y), where the first number represents the x-coordinate and the second number represents the y-coordinate.

Math for the Ages

This game is suitable for all ages, but some supervision for the youngest crowd might be needed.

Eating Cards

Use a deck of cards to learn about inequalities.

Algebra Concept: Inequalities (less than, greater than, and equal to)

From the Junk Drawer:

☐ Scissors   ☐ Tape or glue

☐ Paper   ☐ Deck of playing cards (or dice)

☐ Green marker

Step 1: Cut six strips of paper about ¾ inch by 3 inches. Cut little *v*'s into one side of all six strips, as shown. You are going to be making three alligators.

Step 2: Color the top part of each strip green. Leave the jagged part white to represent the teeth of your gators.

Step 3: Connect two of the gator mouths as shown. Cut little circles and draw a dot in the center for eyes. Tape or glue the eyes as shown. You have created a greater-than gator, a less-than gator, and an equal-to gator.

Step 4: Remove all of the face cards from a deck of cards. With the remaining deck, deal out two cards and leave a space between them. Decide which of the inequalities (or the equal sign) goes between the two cards. Because the alligator is hungry, it always wants to eat the larger number—its mouth should open toward the higher card. If the cards appear as shown, you would say, "Three is less than eight."

Step 5: If the larger number is on the left, you would say, "Eight is greater than three."

Step 6: If the numbers are equal, place the equal sign between the two. (The gator doesn't know which card to eat.)

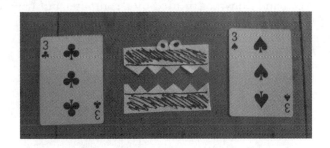

The Math Behind It

Inequalities are a key component of algebra. Less than and greater than are easy enough to understand with the hungry gator. Of course, sometimes the numbers will be equal.

Math for the Ages

This activity is appropriate for all ages but is particularly useful for young mathematicians and struggling older mathematicians. Also, adding an art project to a math class is never a bad thing.

File Folder Battleship

Use file folders and the classic kid's game Battleship to learn about cartesian coordinates.

Algebra Concept: Coordinates

From the Junk Drawer:

☐ 4 pieces of paper
☐ Marker or pen
☐ Ruler
☐ Tape

☐ 2 file folders
☐ 10 paperclips of various sizes(or colored paper "ships")
☐ Scissors

Step 1: Draw a 10-by-10 grid on two sheets of paper. Number the lines on the grid paper 0, 1, 2, 3, etc., up to 10. Label the *x*-**axis** and *y*-**axis**. These grids could be hand drawn or printed on a computer, but hand drawn will allow you to use different colors and a creative touch. You can use a ruler or just draw freehand.

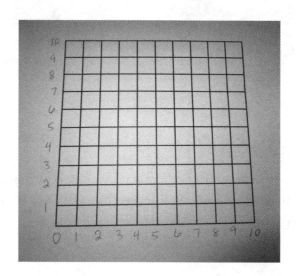

Step 2: Tape the two grids to the inside of a file folder. You can use big and little paperclips for ships. In a classroom, three big clips and two small clips is a good mix. Or you can create five ships from scrap paper. The ships can be any length, but both teams must have the same size and number of ships. (The actual game of Battleship has a five-length ship, a four, two threes, and a two-length ship.) Repeat Steps 1 and 2 so you have two game boards.

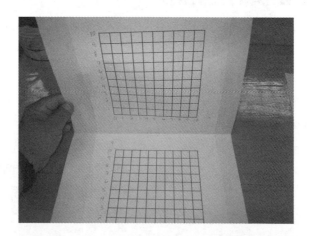

Step 3: Place your ships along the lines (this is different than the game). Remember to hide your ships from your opponent's view.

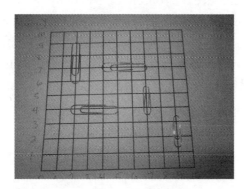

Step 4: Call out *x-y* coordinates to sink the ships. Mark on the top grid with the coordinates you call out, and use the bottom grid for the coordinates your opponent calls out. Use *O*s for misses and *X*s for hits. When all the coordinates beneath a ship have been called, the player must announce that his or her ship has been sunk. Keep playing until one player has sunk all five of the opponent's ships.

The Math Behind It

Understanding the *x-y* coordinate system is essential to the graphing element of algebra. Coordinates are commonly written in the form (x,y). The first number is the number on the *x*-axis (horizontal) and the second number is the number up the *y*-axis (vertical). The spot where the two numbers meet is the actual point on the graph.

Math for the Ages

This is a fun way to reinforce the concept of x-y coordinates and is appropriate for all ages from elementary up. Teachers could photocopy and laminate grids and ships to create a set of games that could easily be stored in a file cabinet. Students would then write on the laminated surfaces with dry-erase markers, so the grids could be wiped clean. Teachers could also just print off 10-by-10 grids but let the students number and color them. Always recycle the paper when done.

Lucky Graphs

Use Lucky Charms cereal to practice bar graphs.

Algebra Concepts: Probability, and bar graphs

From the Junk Drawer:

☐ Small bowl

☐ Lucky Charms cereal

☐ Paper plate or paper towel (optional)

☐ Paper

☐ Pencil or pen

Step 1: Start with a small bowl full of Lucky Charms (without milk). Sort the Lucky Charms into all of the different shapes and colors possible. If you do this on a paper plate or a paper towel, it keeps the cereal clean, so it can be "disposed of" later.

Step 2: On a piece of paper, write all of the shapes down the left-hand side. Including both cereal and marshmallow pieces, there are 12 (or 13) different shapes in most boxes: 8 (or 9) marshmallow shapes, and 4 cereal-piece shapes. Line up the cereal pieces from left to right to make a horizontal bar graph.

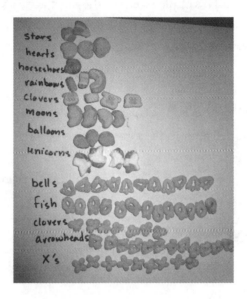

Step 3: Draw a bar graph to show how many of each piece were in your sample.

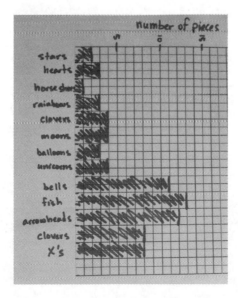

The Math Behind It

Bar graphs are the first type of graphs most students learn. They are useful and simple. They can be used to study sorting, counting, and probability. The probability of getting a certain shape would be equal to the number of that shape divided by the total sample size. For the most accurate numbers, you can combine an entire classroom's worth of data. Probability is a concept taught in middle school math and then explored in most Algebra 2 classrooms.

Math for the Ages

This activity is fun for all ages and is a great way to introduce younger students to graphing. In a larger group setting, you can use this graph to compare to other groups. You can also use this to study the probability of getting a certain shape.

Multiples of 3

Any number whose digits add up to a **factor** of 3 is divisible by 3.

Algebra Concept: Factors

From the Junk Drawer:

☐ Cereal pieces (or paper clips, pennies, poker chips, etc.)

Step 1: Chose a number whose digits add up to a factor of 3, such as 63, 54, 36, etc., and count out that number of cereal pieces. For example, start with 27 pieces of cereal. Split the cereal into place values: 20 and 7.

Step 2: Split the 20 into groups of 10. Ask yourself the question, "What is the easiest way to get each group of 10 into a number divisible by 3?"

Step 3: Remove one piece of cereal from each 10 pile. Now you have 9 left in each pile, which is divisible by 3. You will be left with 2 removed pieces to combine with the 7 left from earlier. Together they add up to 9, which is divisible by 3. All numbers that are multiples of 3 work for this activity, it just depends on how much cereal you want to use. Try it with another two-digit number whose digits add up to a multiple of 3.

The Math Behind It

The Multiples of 3 trick is well known in math circles. This cereal trick is a fun way to visualize it. Taking one away from each 10 stack leaves 9 (divisible by 3). The single cereal pieces removed and the leftovers from the initial number always add up to a number that is divisible by 3.

The trick still works with larger values (such as three-digit numbers). Separate the cereal pieces into place-value blocks—hundreds, tens, and leftover ones. Taking one cereal piece away from each 100 block leaves you with 99, which is divisible by 3. Taking one piece away from each 10 block leaves you with 9, which is divisible by 3. Add the single pieces you took away to the left-over ones, and you will have a multiple of 3.

Math for the Ages

This activity could be done with any age. It may even be a great way to introduce factors to young elementary-age students. Advanced students could be asked to mathematically prove why it works. This is a great idea for a Fun Math Friday event for all ages. Many students know this trick already, but this is a tasty way to learn it for those who don't know.

Multiplication Battle

Use a deck of cards and a friend to practice multiplication tables.

Algebra Concept: Multiplication tables

From the Junk Drawer:

☐ Deck of cards

Step 1: Start with an ordinary deck of cards. (You can remove the face cards if you want or leave them in and count each as 10.) Deal half of the cards to each person.

To play, each person should lay one card face up in the middle of the table (or floor) at the same time. To get the cards, the players multiply the cards together. The first person to say the correct answer gets both cards.

Step 2: After all the cards have been played, count each player's cards. Whoever has the most cards is the winner.

The Math Behind It

Knowing your multiplication tables is crucial to success in algebra. Multiplication facts just take memorization. The more practice you get, the better you will know your multiplication facts.

Math for the Ages

This is a fun way to practice multiplication skills. Teachers or parents can play with students and can even lose on purpose to increase the student's confidence.

Multiply Using Lines

Use this cool hands-on way to learn to multiply.

Algebra Concept: Multiplication

From the Junk Drawer:

☐ Paper (or whiteboard)   ☐ Calculator (optional)

☐ Pencil (or dry-erase marker)

Step 1: Pick a simple two-digit number to multiply by another two-digit number. This example uses 12 and 14.

Start by drawing one angled line, as shown, to represent the tens digit in 12. Leave a space, then draw two angled lines to represent the ones digit in 12. Together, these lines represent the number 12.

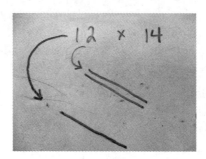

Step 2: Use a similar method to represent 14. Draw one angled line slanting in the other direction, as shown, to represent the tens digit in 14. Leave a space and draw four lines parallel to the line you just drew to represent the ones digit in 14. Together these lines represent the number 14.

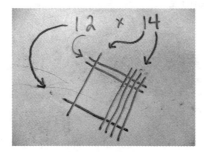

Step 3: Now "separate" the diagram into sections by drawing two curved lines as shown.

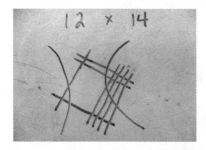

Step 4: Starting on the right side, count the number of intersections you have in that section only. For our example, we had eight intersections. This represents the number 8 in the ones column.

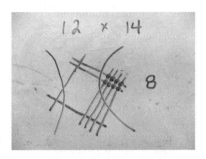

Step 5: Now count the number of intersections in the center section. For this example, there are six intersections in the center section. This represents six groups of 10. Repeat for the left section. For this example, there is one intersection in the left section. This represents one group of 100.

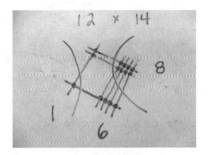

Step 6: Write the numbers in order by place value to get your solution. For this example, the answer is 168. You can check it with a calculator.

If you count more than nine digits in any section, you will need to need to do more work to get your answer, as shown in Steps 7 through 11.

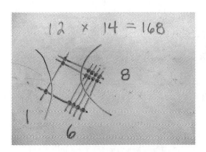

Step 7: When your multiplied numbers have digits that are greater than 5, you will need to move a few numbers to get the correct answer. To start, draw the lines just as shown earlier. This example uses 13 and 27.

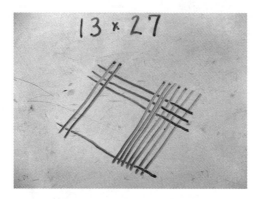

Step 8: Now create the sections as you did before.

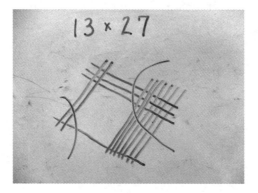

Step 9: Count the number of intersections in each section and write them down. In this example, there are 2, 13, and 21 intersections, respectively.

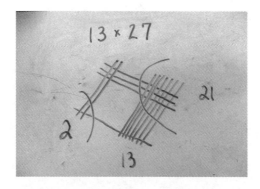

Step 10: Take the 2 away from the 21 and add it to the center section number. (You are moving 20 to the tens place.)

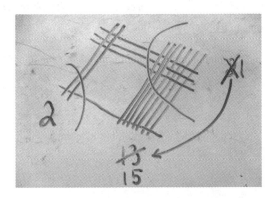

Step 11: You now have 15 in the tens place. Take the 1 (which represents 10 groups of 10, or 100) and move it to the hundreds place.

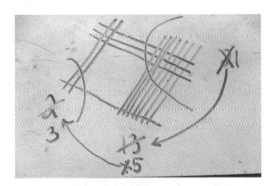

Step 12: Now, write the numbers in order by place value. For this example, the answer is 351. Double-check with a calculator or by hand.

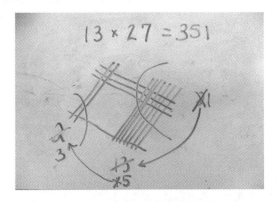

Step 13: If you have a 0 in one of your numbers, there is a trick to using it. This example uses 12 and 10. Draw **integers** as solid lines, but draw a 0 as a wiggly line. *Nothing that intersects with a wiggly line will count,* since multiplying any number by 0 equals 0.

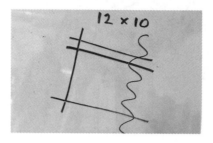

Step 14: In this example, when you count the number of intersections in each section, you will get the number 120. Remember, never count any intersection that contains a wiggly line.

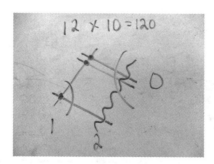

Step 15: You can even do larger numbers, but the diagram needs to be drawn bigger. Draw hundred lines, skip some space, draw tens lines, skip some space, then draw ones lines. Repeat for the other number at the opposite angle.

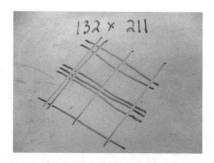

Step 16: Section the diagram off, but now you will have five sections as shown. Count the number of intersections in each section. Carry any numbers over, if needed, as shown in Steps 10 and 11. Write down the number; this is your final answer. You could even multiply bigger numbers if you had a bigger piece of paper (or whiteboard).

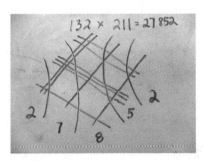

The Math Behind It

Multiplying by lines is often called *Japanese multiplication*, *Vedic multiplication*, or *Indian multiplication*, though no one is completely sure where this method came from.

The process works because the lines accurately represent place value. This method is really no different than using hundreds blocks, tens blocks, and ones blocks, which is a common way of teaching multiplication today. The best explanation can be viewed using a picture.

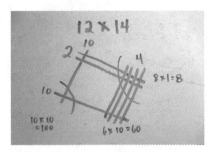

For the number 12, the lowest line represents a ten line and the highest lines represent single digits. For the number 14, the left line represents a ten line and the right lines represent single digits. The right section has eight intersections and all of those lines represent 1×1, so you get 8 in the ones place.

The middle section has six intersections, but each line represents 1 × 10. So the middle section represents 60. The left section has one intersection of one ten line and another ten line (10 × 10), so it equals 100. Put 100, 60, and 8 together and you have 168, the correct answer.

Math for the Ages

This activity is suitable from elementary age and up. It would make a great inquiry-based activity for advanced students. Show them how it works and let them explore other examples.

Nine-Finger Trick

Learn the key to multiplying by 9 using only nine fingers.
Algebra Concept: Multiplication

From the Junk Drawer:

☐ 2 hands

Step 1: Hold your hands in front of you with your palms facing up. To multiply 4 × 9, fold down the fourth finger from the left. The answer is 36. Look at your fingers, you have three to the left of the bent finger and six to the right of the bent finger.

Step 2: Try 7 × 9 . . . six to the left and three to the right. The answer is 63!

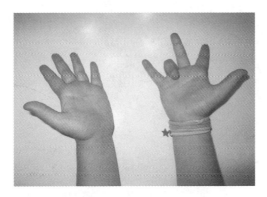

Step 3: If you are showing this trick to someone else and your palms are facing them, his or her left will be your right. To show 4 × 6 to someone else, you need to fold down the fourth finger *from the right*. It will look correct from the other person's point of view (but backward to you).

The Math Behind It

You have 10 fingers. Since 9 is 1 less than 10, every finger you put down equals 1 taken away from each 10. So 4 × 9 means you have taken away 4 from 40 and you are left with 36.

Math for the Ages

This activity is appropriate for middle elementary age and up, because that is when students start multiplication. Younger students could do this activity to get a head start. In a classroom setting, some students will know this trick already, but many won't. There are even high school students who have never seen this.

Perfect Squares Are Odd

Use sticky notes (or toilet paper) to learn a really cool math fact.

Algebra Concepts: **Perfect squares,** and **parabolas**

From the Junk Drawer:
☐ Sticky notes (or toilet paper squares)   ☐ Marker
☐ Large, flat surface

Step 1: Place one sticky note on a large, flat surface (you might want to use the floor).

Next to that sticky note, place four more as shown. (You could also do this with toilet paper squares if you have a large enough floor space.) There are also very small sticky notes if you want to do this on a tabletop.

Step 2: Continue by adding the next two perfect squares: 9 and 16. The paper squares will form a parabola if you look at the shape created only by the

top of each stack. You could continue beyond 16 with 25, 36, etc., if you choose, but you can see the pattern with 1 through 16.

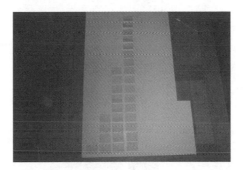

Step 3: Look at the difference between the length of each column; you will see a very cool math fact. Color in the squares that are *above* the previous column, as shown. Successive perfect squares are separated by consecutive odd integers: 1, 3, 5, 7, etc.

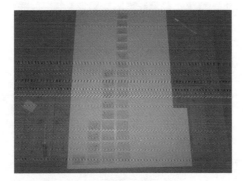

Step 4: This is an alternative way to see the same pattern using toilet paper. Start by laying one square of toilet paper on your work surface, and next to that, four squares. It is easiest if you count the number of squares while keeping the strips intact.

Step 5: Next, add a column of 9 and a column of 16. Of course, you can continue the pattern if you have a large enough area.

Step 6: Tear off the squares that are above the column to their left. For example, tear off three squares from the 4 column, tear off five squares from the 9 column, etc.

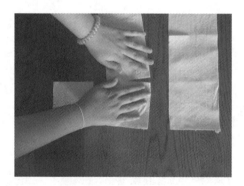

Step 7: Take the squares you tore from each column and place them next to each other. You should see a pattern of 1, 3, 5, 7, etc. Again, the perfect squares are separated by consecutive odd integers.

The Math Behind It

Parabolas are a beautiful natural shape. The basic formula for a parabola is $y = mx^2$. Across the bottom of your graph are integers, and above each integer is the perfect square of that number. Though it looks like a bar graph, it is also similar to a coordinate plot. The m in the **equation** simply shows how steep the parabola is. The m for your parabola is 1.

The fact that perfect squares are separated by consecutive odd numbers was known to ancient mathematicians. The pattern goes on forever.

Math for the Ages

This is a great way to introduce parabolas to all ages. It also allows them to see a cool math pattern. This activity in a classroom also gets students out of their seats, another good thing—math needs to be active when it can be. And it is fun to learn math from toilet paper.

Positive and Negative Candy

This activity is a tasty way to teach adding positive and negative numbers for struggling learners.

Algebra Concept: Adding negative and positive numbers

From the Junk Drawer:

☐ Candies, 2 different colors (or different tokens such as pennies and nickels)

☐ Paper and pencil (or whiteboard and dry-erase marker)

Step 1: Choose one color candy (or other object) to represent positive numbers and a different color (or other object) to represent negative numbers. On a piece of paper (or whiteboard), write your math problem. This example uses $4 + (-2) = $ ___. Beneath the 4, place four "positive" pieces of candy. Beneath the 2, place two "negative" pieces of candy.

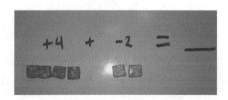

Step 2: Leave an equal number of candies under each number—they cancel each other out. Move the "extra" candies to the other side of the equal sign.

For this example, you ended up with two extra positive candies; the answer is +2. For a positive value, it is customary not to write the plus sign, but when you are first learning about negative numbers, it is a good idea to write it.

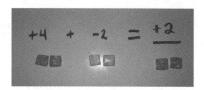

Step 3: Try another example. The example shown is −5 + 3 = ___. Place five negative candies under −5 and three positive candies under 3.

Step 4: Move the extra candies to the other side of the equal sign. You have two extra negative candies, so the answer is −2.

The Math Behind It

Positive and negative numbers are key to algebra. Positive numbers can be shown on a number line as numbers to the right of zero. Negative numbers would be found to the left of the zero. Adding positive and negative numbers is the first concept that students need to grasp when learning about numbers of opposite signs. The concept needs to be understood before they go on to other mathematical functions like multiplication and division of numbers with opposite signs.

Math for the Ages

This is a concept traditionally taught in middle elementary school grades, but it can be understood at an early age, especially with a hands-on method like this. This activity would be a great way to first introduce the topic. It is also a great way to help older learners who are struggling with opposite signs or to help special needs children understand this concept.

The Sounds of Math

Hear a perfect square in action.

Algebra Concepts: Perfect squares, and parabolas

From the Junk Drawer:
- ☐ 8-foot piece of clothesline cord
- ☐ 9 binder clips
- ☐ Ruler (or yardstick)
- ☐ Several books
- ☐ Cookie sheet
- ☐ Sturdy chair

Step 1: Start with an 8-foot piece of clothesline cord. Tie a knot in one end. Put binder clips at the following distances (all perfect squares) from the knot: 1 inch, 4 inches, 9 inches, 16 inches, 25 inches, 36 inches, 49 inches, 64 inches, and 81 inches. Thicker string works a little better with binder clips, which are easy to position and have a decent amount of weight. Thinner string works well, but you will have to tie the weights on. Fishing weights, paper clips, and metal nuts all work well if you tie them on thinner string.

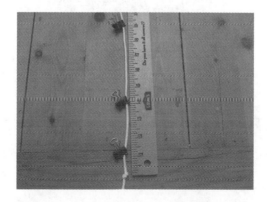

Step 2: Use a few books to lift a cookie sheet at angle to the ground.

Step 3: A sturdy chair is helpful for the next part, since the chair allows you to reach a little higher. Hold the top of the string in the air. Move it up or down until the knot lightly rests on the cookie sheet.

Step 4: Let go of the top and listen to the sounds created. You might have to repeat it a few times to clearly hear the Sounds of Math.

The Math Behind It

Objects fall because of gravity. The distance an object falls is related to the square of the time: that is, if an object falls a distance in one second, it will fall four times the distance in two seconds. The distances of the binder clips on the clothesline are all perfect squares: 1, 4, 9, 16, and so on. Since the distances are perfect squares and gravity causes objects to fall related to the square of the time, the pings are an equal distance apart. What you hear is a parabola in action. As you learn more about parabolas, you will find out what a wonderful curved shape they are.

Math for the Ages

This is appropriate for all ages. It makes a great inquiry lab for older students. Give them the distances and have them create the string-weight combination. After they drop the string, allow them to come up with the fact that the equation for falling objects leads to a parabola.

Squares Are Easy

Learn a super cool trick to calculate perfect squares. Note: this activity assumes the single-digit perfect squares are known—for example, 3 squared equals 9, 5 squared equals 25, and so on.

Algebra Concept: Perfect squares

From the Junk Drawer:

☐ Paper and pencil or whiteboard and   ☐ Calculator
   dry-erase marker

Step 1: Write a two-digit number between 11 and 19 on your piece of paper (or whiteboard) and square it. This example uses 14. Next, figure out how far away your number is from 10. (In this case, 14 is 4 away from 10.)

Step 2: Use the number you got in Step 1 (in this example, 4) and subtract it from your original number. Next, add the number from Step 1 to your original number.

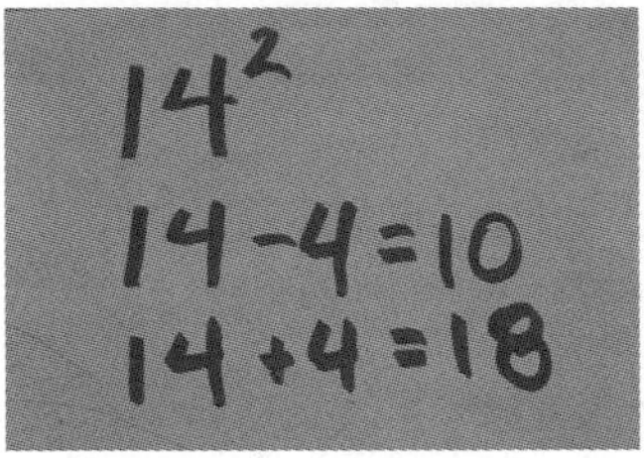

$$14^2$$
$$14 - 4 = 10$$
$$14 + 4 = 18$$

Step 3: Multiply the results together.

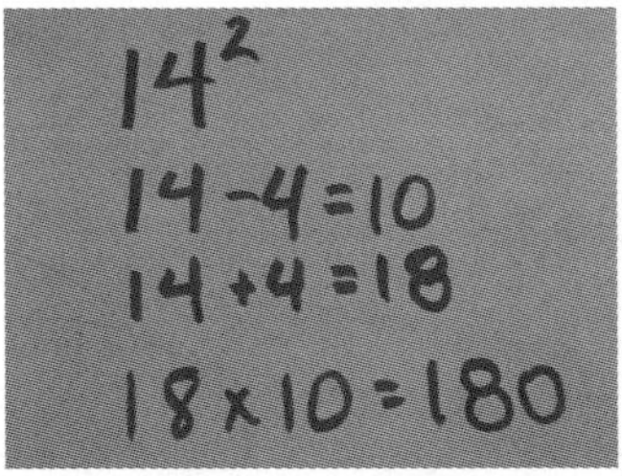

$$14^2$$
$$14 - 4 = 10$$
$$14 + 4 = 18$$
$$18 \times 10 = 180$$

Step 4: Take the number you got in Step 1 (4 in this example) and square it. Add the Step 3 answer to this number and you have the square of your original number. You can double-check it with a calculator.

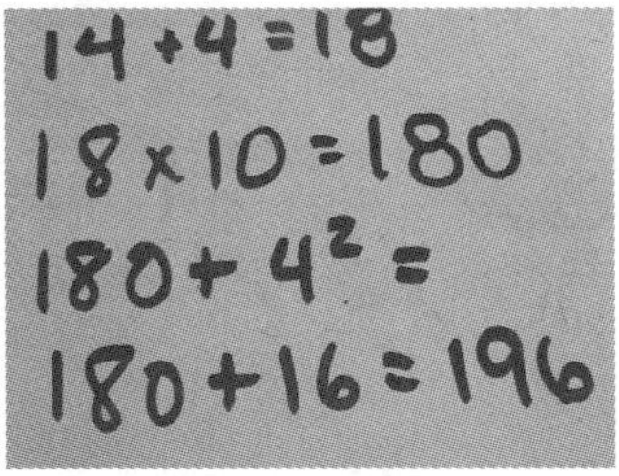

$$14 + 4 = 18$$
$$18 \times 10 = 180$$
$$180 + 4^2 =$$
$$180 + 16 = 196$$

The Math Behind It

Math has many tricks and this is only one. Math brains have known these tricks for years. Another way to approach the same problem is to write it as shown in the following example and use factoring to split the 14 up. For example, 14 × 14 = (10 + 4) × (10 + 4). Using **FOIL** (first, outside, inside, last), that's 100 + 40 + 40 + 16 = 196.

This method can be built upon to square three-digit numbers, four-digit numbers, and greater numbers of digits, but a calculator might become easier at some point.

Math for the Ages

This activity is appropriate for upper elementary and above. For high achievers, the solution could be left out. Let them figure it out themselves. Also, high achievers may want to try three- and four-digit numbers.

Toothpick Pi

Toss toothpicks to find the value of **pi** (π).

Algebra Concept: Pi

From the Junk Drawer:

☐ Toothpicks
☐ Ruler
☐ Large sheet of paper (or whiteboard)

☐ Marker (or masking tape)
☐ Flat area

Step 1: Create a table with a place to mark tosses and crosses. First, measure the length of a toothpick. Create five long lines that are separated by the length of the toothpick on a large sheet of paper (or a whiteboard) as shown. The lines should be skinny but visible.

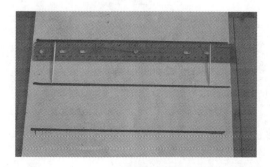

Step 2: Start with a certain number of toothpicks (20 or so). Drop the toothpicks on the marked area. Count the total number of toothpicks tossed, then count the number of toothpicks that land crossing one of the lines. To count as a cross, the toothpick must completely cross a line. Repeat the process. You need to toss at least 200 toothpicks for best results, so repeat it several times (20 toothpicks ×10 trial drops). Record each trial in your data table.

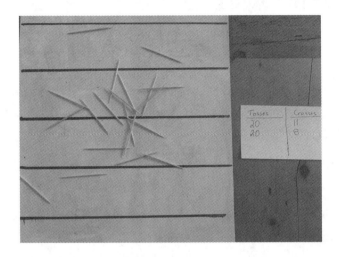

Step 3: Multiply the number of tosses by 2. Divide that number by the number of toothpick "crosses" and you will get extremely close to the value of pi.

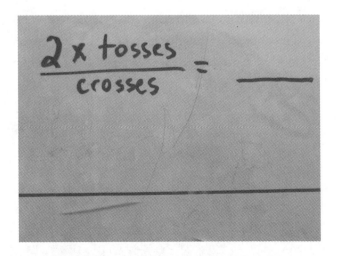

The Math Behind It

This activity is a probability activity first explained in 1777 and is called the Buffon needle experiment. The Comte de Buffon used needles and parallel lines, but toothpicks are far safer. (The activity can also be done with pencils on the floor using masking tape for the lines.) The experiment was one of the first to be used in geometric probability. In other words, the chance of something happening depends on the geometry of the shape. The math is fairly complex and actually crosses into the world of complex trigonometry and calculus. Though calculating pi using this method is a geometry (and probability) activity, it can be helpful in algebra because pi is useful in math. It also helps a little bit with statistics. The number of tosses is the independent variable, because you control the number of tosses. The number of crosses is the dependent variable, because the number of crosses depends on the number of tosses.

Math for the Ages

This is safe for any age and fun. Attempting the tosses at least 200 times is also a good way to reinforce the process that math must be repeatable. Advanced students could research the Buffon needle experiment and look into why it works. In a classroom, each person or group could do the calculation and then use the data from the entire class to get closer to pi.

2

Algebra Tools

A lgebra is fun, but sometimes difficult. Math comes to everyone at different speeds. The algebra tools in this chapter will help students understand the math faster. Hands-on activities are a good way to visually understand the subject.

Have fun while you use these tools. But be careful, you just might learn something.

A Box Plot of Cards

Use playing cards to create a **box plot** diagram.

Algebra Concept: Box plot diagrams (also called *box and whisker diagrams*)

From the Junk Drawer:
☐ Deck of cards
☐ Pencil and paper (or whiteboard and dry-erase marker)

Step 1: Remove all of the face cards from a deck of cards. Draw seven cards from the deck randomly and arrange them from largest value to smallest. Seven cards fit on the whiteboard shown, but any number greater than four would work.

Step 2: Flip over the outside cards two at a time so they are face down, until you are left with a single middle card face up, if you started with an odd number, or two cards face up, if you started with an even number. If a single card remains face up, that is your **median**. If you used an even number of cards, the median would be the average of the two cards left face up in the middle. Draw a number line from 1 to 10. Draw a line below the number line, making the median value.

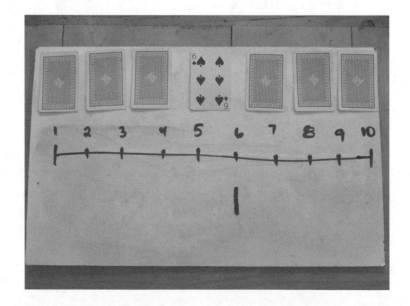

Step 3: Flip the higher half of the cards (rounded up) face up. If you used an odd number of cards, this will be the median and everything higher. If you used an even number of cards, this will be the higher of the two cards used to calculate your median and everything above that. Then, turn the highest and lowest of these cards face down in pairs until you have only one or two cards remaining face up, as shown.

This card or the average of these two cards is called the *upper quartile*. This number represents the median of the higher values. Draw a line on the number line below this value, as shown.

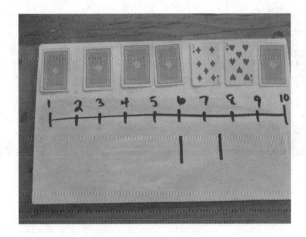

Step 4: Repeat Step 3 with the lower half of the cards. This leaves you with one or two cards face up, as shown. The one card left face up or the average of the two cards left face up is called the *lower quartile*. This is the median of the lower values. Draw a line on the number line below this value, as shown.

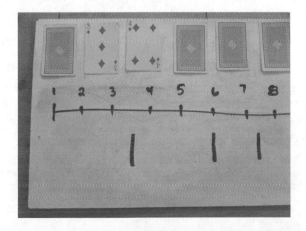

Step 5: Draw a line across the top and bottom of the lines you just drew to make a box. And finally, flip over the outermost cards. Draw a line below the value of each of these cards. Now, draw straight lines from the sides of your box to these lines. These are called the "whiskers."

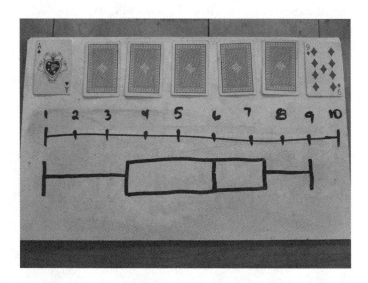

Step 6: To help remember the concept, you can make the center box into a cat. The whiskers of a cat are as wide as its body. So if the whiskers fit in an opening, the cat's body can fit too. The whiskers of your box plot represent the farthest reaches of your data.

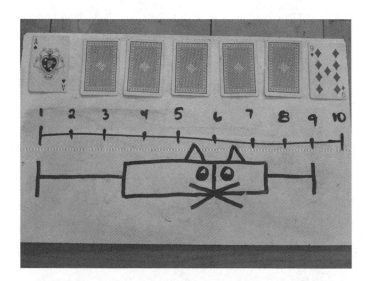

The Math Behind It

Box plots are a way to show measured data on a graph. The middle line in the box represents the median for the values. The right side of the box represents the median of the top half of the data (the upper quartile). The left side of the box represents the median for the bottom half of the data (the lower quartile). The "whiskers" extend to the extremes of the data.

Box plots are a very useful way to see how well data points agree. Box plots are useful in drawing a **line of best fit** for graphed data. Often in algebra, you start with a function and graph it, but real-life data, like the card values pulled from a deck, can be used to create a function.

Some mathematicians say to remove outliers from the data. Outliers are data points that are very far removed from every other value. In my classroom, outliers are left in, but students are asked to explain what might have led to these far-from-median results.

Math for the Ages

Box plots can be drawn by students of all ages. A fun way to draw them is to create two small triangles on top of the box. Add a few eyes and you have a rectangular cat face. The whiskers extending out to the sides makes it easy for students to remember that whiskers represent the extremes of the data.

In a classroom, a great way to teach box plots is by using the heights of all the students. Line them up from short to tall, measure, and then draw a box plot on the board. Any group of measurements can be used to create box plots. My students shot rubber bands with their names on them one year. Of course, they were shooting them down the hall from a starting point, not at each other.

Box plots are often drawn vertically, not horizontally. The math is still the same. Learning box plots in a horizontal direction just seems to make it easier for students.

Checkerboard Coordinates

Learn the meaning of ordered pairs with an old checkerboard.

Algebra Concept: Coordinates (and ordered pairs)

From the Junk Drawer:

☐ Checkerboard   ☐ Checkers

☐ Sticky notes   ☐ Index cards

☐ Marker (optional)   ☐ Pen or pencil

Step 1: The bottom edge of a checkerboard will be the *x*-axis, and the side edge will be the *y*-axis. Using sticky notes, label each axis with 0, 1, 2, 3, etc., up to 8, as shown. This grid will be used to teach students to visualize the meaning of (x,y) ordered pairs, sometimes referred to as coordinates.

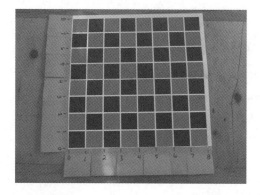

Step 2: Place a checker at (1,2), which is one line over and two lines up on the checkerboard.

Step 3: Using index cards, create a set of flashcards with various *x-y* coordinates on them. On the back of the card, draw a sketch to show where the checker should be placed.

For practice, draw a card at random and place a checker on that point.

Step 4: Turn the card over to check and see if you are correct.

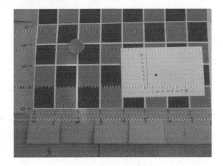

The Math Behind It

Coordinate systems are fundamental to understanding graphing and algebra. The standard format for writing ordered pairs is (x,y). The first number is the x-location and the second number is the y-location. In three-dimensional space, there is even a third coordinate for a z-location.

Math for the Ages

This is a great way to introduce coordinates (ordered pairs) and is really suitable for all ages. For teachers, checkerboards make great coordinate axes, and checkers make great markers for ordered pairs. Many people have old checkers games they are willing to donate. The boards fold and are easy to store. If they are going to be used in a classroom permanently, use tape or write on the boards to label the axes. Even after they are written on, they can still be used to play checkers. Most dollar stores sell checkers games with cardboard game boards that are perfect if you want a class set.

The game of checkers is actually a good strategy game, so having a set in your classroom for students to use after they finish their work is a good way to have the boards do double duty.

Distribute This

Learn the **distributive property** using old blocks.

Algebra Concept: Distributive property

From the Junk Drawer:

☐ Old set of baby blocks
☐ Blank address labels
☐ Marker

☐ Binder clips
☐ Paper (or whiteboard)
☐ Pen (or dry-erase marker)

Step 1: Create number blocks from old baby blocks. Use the blank address labels to put the numbers 1 through 6 on different sides of a block. Repeat for at least four blocks. Put the numbers 7 through 12 on different sides of another four blocks.

Step 2: In this activity, binder clips will be used to represent *x*, the unknown in the equation. The blocks are used for the numbers.

Write a simple equation on paper or a whiteboard. The example shown is 2 (x + 2) = 6. Place the corresponding blocks and binder clips below the equation.

Step 3: Remove the initial 2 and expand the equation using additional binder clips and blocks. The 2 on the outside of the parentheses means that there are two of everything inside the parentheses. So add a second binder clip and a second number 2 block. By doing this, you are *distributing* the 2 inside the parentheses.

Step 4: Combine the two number blocks into a new value by adding the numbers and replacing both with a single number block (4).

Step 5: Subtract the lower number block (4) from both sides of the equation and replace the larger number (6) with a new block (2). The smaller number block will disappear since you are taking a number and subtracting the same number, resulting in 0.

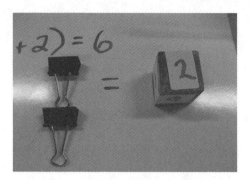

Step 6: Divide both sides by the number of clips to get the answer for the unknown. You may end up with a fraction as your answer—that is OK.

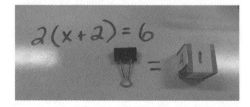

The Math Behind It

The distributive property is invaluable to algebra. Algebra uses variables in equations to solve for unknowns. This property becomes fundamental to solving equations. Being able to see the distributive property in action helps many students.

Math for the Ages

This is a great topic to master at home before it is needed in the classroom. Even elementary-age students will get this, once they have begun to master simple multiplication.

Factorial Cards

Use playing cards to learn about **factorials**.

Algebra Concept: Factorials

From the Junk Drawer:

☐ Deck of cards   ☐ Calculator

Step 1 Separate a deck of cards into the four different suits—diamonds, clubs, hearts, and spades. Arrange the cards in numeric order from 1 (the ace) to 10. Set all of the face cards to the side.

Step 2: Pick the first three cards in a set to use as an example. Arrange the cards in descending order, with the highest value on the left. This will represent 3. Mathematicians read "3!" as "3 factorial." The value of 3! is 3 × 2 × 1. Plug it into a calculator to get the answer (6). Return the cards to the stack when you are finished and place them back in numerical order.

Step 3: Now, pick the first six cards in a set. Lay them out in descending order and calculate 6! with a calculator (720). Put the cards back in numeric order when you are finished.

For additional practice, pick a random number of cards. Lay them out and calculate the factorial of the highest number.

The Math Behind It

Factorials are used in statistics and in higher levels of math. One common use of factorials is in the probability of something happening. Let's say you have four friends waiting in a line. There are 4! possibilities of how they could be arranged in line. And 4! is equal to 24. There are 24 different possible arrangements for four people standing in line:

ABCD, ABDC, ACBD, ACDB, ADBC, ADCB, BACD, BADC, BCAD, BCDA, BDAC, BDCA, CABD, CADB, CBAD, CBDA, CDAB, CDBA, DABC, DACB, DBAC, DBCA, DCAB, and DCBA.

Math for the Ages

Factorials are traditionally taught at the high school level, and the subjects that use them are primarily high school and/or college level. But the concept is easy enough to understand after students learn multiplication. This activity lets the students explore the factorial in an easy manner.

One deck of cards would create four factorial sets to use in a classroom. A fun way to use this is to play the Four Fours puzzle. For this, create a + card, a − card, a × card, a ÷ card, a √ card, and a ! card. Every number from 1 to 100 can be made using only four number 4s and all of the different mathematical operations (addition, multiplication, factorials, **square roots,** etc.).

FOILed Again

Use aluminum foil to learn how to multiply **polynomials** using the FOIL method.

Algebra Concept: FOIL method of multiplying polynomials

From the Junk Drawer:

☐ Paper and pencil (or whiteboard and dry-erase marker)

☐ Aluminum foil

Step 1: Write out two polynomials to be multiplied on a piece of paper or whiteboard. Any two polynomials will do. This example uses $(x - 6)(x + 3)$.

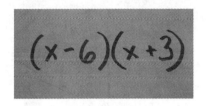

Step 2: First, multiply the first (F) terms in each polynomial. Take a thin strip of aluminum foil and connect the two first terms. Write a large F over the foil to help you remember *first terms*. Write the product of the two terms beneath the polynomials and foil strips.

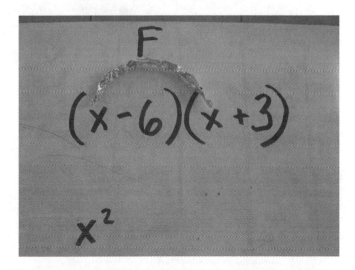

Step 3: The next step is to multiply the outside (O) terms in each polynomial. Take a thin strip of aluminum foil and connect the outside terms. Write a large O over the foil to help you remember *outside terms*. Write the product of the two terms beneath the polynomials and foil strips and add the terms.

Step 4: Next, multiply the inside (I) terms in each polynomial. Take a thin strip of aluminum foil and connect the inside terms. Write a large I over the foil to help you remember *inside terms*. Write the product of the two terms beneath the polynomials and foil strips. You are still adding terms, but now you are adding a $-6x$, which is the same as subtracting $6x$.

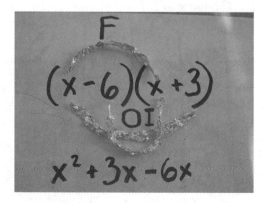

Step 5: The final step is to multiply the last (L) terms in each polynomial. Take a thin strip of aluminum foil and connect the last terms. Write a large L over the foil to help you remember *last terms*. Write the product

of the two terms beneath the polynomials and foil strips. You are again adding the terms, but adding -18 is the same as subtracting 18.

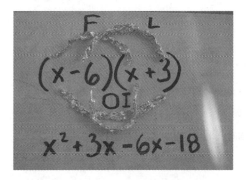

Simplify similar terms and you have the answer: $(x - 6)(x + 3) = x2 - 3x - 18$.

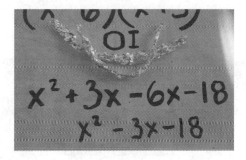

The Math Behind It

The FOIL method is the most common way of teaching students how to multiply polynomials. FOIL is a mnemonic device to help you remember all of the steps: **f**irst, **o**utside, **i**nside, **l**ast. Multiplying polynomials is one of the first skills taught in algebra. And if you master the first skills, the rest gets easier.

Math for the Ages

This is a great hands-on way to help students physically remember the FOIL method. It could be done with almost all ages, even if it is a few years before you take a real algebra class. And students always remember silly ways to learn something, like using real foil to learn the FOIL method.

Foot Pressure

Stomp on graph paper to learn the concept of **pressure** in this fun math activity.

Algebra Concept: Solving for a variable

From the Junk Drawer:

☐ Bathroom scale

☐ 1 sheet of graph paper (1-inch squares are best)

☐ Pencil or pen

Step 1: Weigh yourself on a bathroom scale. After you know your weight, lightly place your foot on a sheet of graph paper. Trace around the outline of your footprint.

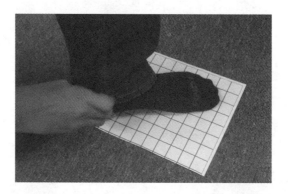

Step 2: Shade in all the 1-inch squares that are *completely* inside your outline.

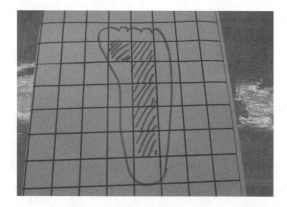

Step 3: Now, estimate how many more square inches you have. The easiest way to do this is to find two partial squares that appear to add up to a full 1-inch square. Keep matching them up—counting as you go along—until you have the total **area** of the bottom of your foot. The number will be in square inches. You can repeat this for the other foot. You might be surprised to see that your feet are slightly different sizes.

Pressure is force divided by area. If you divide your weight by the total areas of both feet, you will get the pressure exerted on the floor by your feet. If you stand on one foot, the pressure on that foot doubles because you now have your total weight acting on only the area of one foot.

The Math Behind It

Solving simple equations where you use letters instead of numbers is important to algebra. The letters are called *variables*. Your variables in this lab were force (your weight) and the area that was in contact with the floor: pressure = force / area. You then get to solve the equation to find the pressure on your feet (or single foot).

Equations are a guide to thinking. Pressure is a science topic, but you need math to understand it. Math is the language for most science courses.

Math for the Ages

This is a great Fun Math Friday activity for all ages. Upper elementary and above can actually add standing on their tiptoes to this lab to feel an even greater pressure. Also, pressure can be used to explain why martial arts are often done with the small side of your hand (e.g., karate chop) and not with your entire fist.

Giant Sand Timers

Create giant sand timers, test them, and graph the results. Different size openings would create graphs with different **slopes**.

Algebra Concepts: Graphing real-world data, and line of best fit

Adult supervision required

From the Junk Drawer:

☐ Superglue

☐ 2 plastic bottles with lids (bottles with smooth sides give the best results)

☐ Drill and bits

☐ Playground sand, beach sand, or salt

☐ Kitchen strainer and bowl (optional, for straining sand)

☐ Funnel

☐ Tape

☐ Ruler

☐ Graph paper

☐ Watch, clock, smartphone, or timer that can measure seconds

Step 1: Superglue two plastic bottle lids together, flat side to flat side. With adult help, drill a ¼-inch hole through the center of the joined lids.

Step 2: If you are using sand, it may need to be sifted to make sure there are no lumps. (This step may not be needed depending on your sand—sand

from a gardening store should have no lumps, but sand from a beach or playground probably will.) You could also do this activity with salt and it would not need sifting.

Step 3: Use a funnel to fill one bottle about three-quarters full with sand.

Step 4: Put the superglued lids on the sand-filled bottle. Wrap tape around the two glued lids to add a little more strength. Electrical tape, clear cellophane tape, and duct tape are all good choices.

Step 5: Attach the bottles by screwing the empty bottle on top of the sand-filled bottle. Tape a ruler to the outside of the empty top bottle. The ruler's 0-inch mark should be at the top of the Giant Sand Timer so it starts measuring once the sand is past any bumps in the bottle's bottom, as shown.

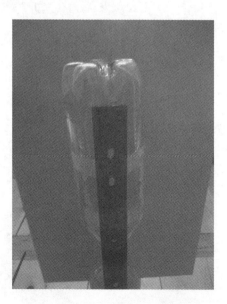

Step 6: Create a table of time (in minutes) and height of sand (in centimeters). Centimeters are the best choice because they are a smaller measurement than inches and it is easier to estimate ⅒ of a centimeter.

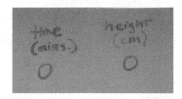

Step 7: Invert the bottles and start timing when the sand reaches the ruler's zero mark. Record your measurements every minute until the sand is all in the bottom. Graph the height of sand in the bottle versus time. Put the time on the *x*-axis and the sand height on the *y*-axis.

Step 8: (Optional) Repeat with larger holes in the lids. You could graph all the values on the same graph using different-colored markers or pencils.

The Math Behind It

Sand timers are one of the oldest timing devices known to mankind. They are also commonly used as timers even today. Many dentists will give you a small sand timer to help you brush your teeth for at least two minutes. The sand falls through the opening at a constant rate. So when it is filling a bottle with flat sides, the graph will be a straight line.

With any recorded data, there is always some variation. So although your graph should be a straight line, some points may not be on that line. That is

OK. Plot all your points, then you will draw a line of best fit. A line of best fit shows you what the general shape of the graph is. Most shapes from natural phenomena are one of several shapes: linear, parabolic, and inverse (hyperbolic). Each individual measurement contains some built-in error, but by using a line of best fit, you average these errors out. The line of best fit is actually more important than the individual points because it balances out the errors.

Math for the Ages

This activity is suitable for all ages with adult help for the superglue and the drill. Small bottles are easier to handle for the younger crowd.

Inverse Pennies

Create an **inverse function** using pennies.

Algebra Concept: Inverse functions

From the Junk Drawer:

☐ Paper and pencil (or whiteboard and dry-erase marker)

☐ Pennies

Step 1: Draw a large *x-y* axis on a piece of paper (or whiteboard). Draw 12 lines, equally spaced out, on the *x*-axis and number every other line.

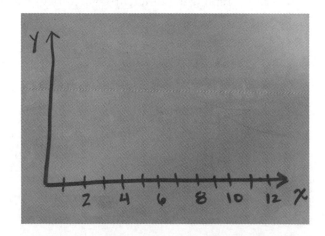

Step 2: Line up 12 pennies over the number 2 line on the *x*-axis. Line up two pennies over the number 12 on the *x*-axis.

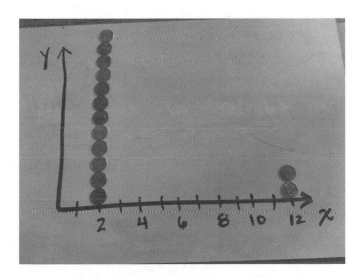

Step 3: Line up eight pennies over the number 3 line on the *x*-axis. Line up three pennies over the number 8. Line up six pennies over the number 4. Line up four pennies over the number 6. The tops of the pennies represent an inverse relationship.

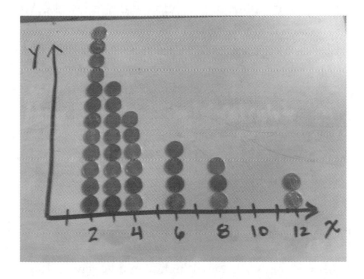

Step 4: As an option, you could remove the top penny and draw a dot where the penny used to be. Connect the dots with a smooth curve to complete a

full inverse relationship graph. Do not connect the dots with straight lines, just draw a smooth freehand line through the points.

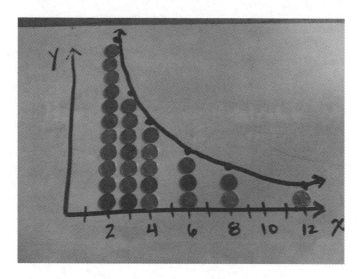

The Math Behind It

An inverse relationship shows that as one variable goes up, the other variable goes down. Inverse relationships are common in the real world. A science example is the pressure and volume of a gas. When the pressure goes up, the volume goes down. Another example is race cars. As the speed of a race car goes up, the time required to complete one lap goes down.

The algebra formula for an inverse relationship is $y = k/x$, where k is a constant. For this example, k was the number 24. When you rearrange the equation, you are left with $y \times x = k$. If you multiply all of the y factors by the corresponding x factor, you always get the number 24. You may want to try other numbers and learn math while using pennies.

Math for the Ages

Inverse relationships are usually taught in late middle school. This activity is fast and appropriate for this age and up. This activity could be done with dried beans to investigate larger values of k.

Line Up

Learn "less than or equal to" and "greater than or equal to" using a scrap piece of plastic.

Algebra Concepts: Less than or equal to, and greater than or equal to

From the Junk Drawer:

☐ Scissors
☐ Piece of clear plastic
☐ Highlighter

☐ Dark permanent marker
☐ Graph paper

Step 1: Cut out a square piece of clear plastic. You can check the recycling bin. Clear (and clean) food containers and the front of toy packages work well. Use a highlighter to color on the plastic. Let the ink dry before handling. Take the dark permanent marker and color along one edge of the plastic.

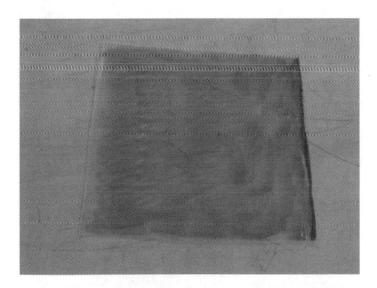

Step 2: Place a piece of graph paper on the table. For this example, you'll use the line $y = 3x + 2$. Place the piece of plastic on the graph paper so that the dark edge is on the line and the colored area is below the dark edge, as shown. This represents the **inequality** $y \leq 3x + 2$. All of the values

in the colored area, including those on the dark line, are solutions to this inequality.

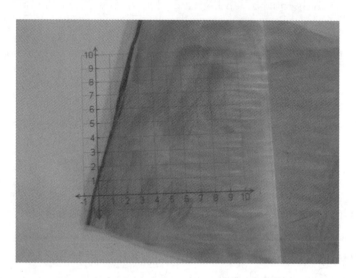

Step 3: Rotate the plastic around so that the black line is not on the graph paper. This represents the inequality $y < 3x + 2$. Now, all of the colored area is a solution for this inequality. But the line $y = 3x + 2$ is not included in the solution because the black line is not shown.

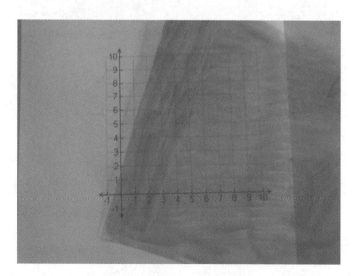

Step 4: Move the plastic so that the dark edge is on the line and the colored area is now above the dark edge, as shown on the next page. This represents

greater than or equal to. The solution shown will be $y \geq 3x + 2$. All of the values in the colored area, including the black line, are solutions to this inequality.

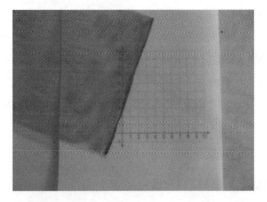

Step 5: Turn the plastic around to represent the inequality $y > 3x + 2$. Now, all of the colored area is a solution. But the line $y = 3x + 2$ is not included in the solution because the black line is not shown.

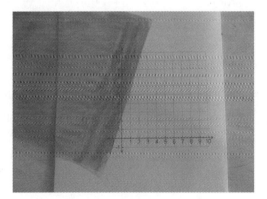

The Math Behind It

Inequalities for functions are critical to the understanding of algebra. With an inequality for a function, you can have many values that are correct. Greater than or less than values do not contain the line (or curve) for the function itself. If you have greater than or equal to, the line (or curve) would be included as part of the solution. Today, high-end graphing calculators even have the ability to color in these inequalities. But a piece of plastic will help you understand it.

Math for the Ages

This is appropriate for upper elementary and older students. By that age, advanced math students are learning functions and the greater than or equal to (and less than or equal to) concept. This would also be great for students in middle and high school if they struggle with this topic. Being able to see less than or equal to in relation to functions may help them comprehend it. The activity also makes it easy for teachers to walk around the room and monitor the students' progress as they practice.

Nickels and Pennies

Use nickels and pennies to learn how to simplify one-variable equations.

Algebra Concept: Simplifying equations

From the Junk Drawer:
☐ Paper and pencil (or whiteboard and dry-erase marker)
☐ Nickels and pennies

Step 1: Write a sample equation on a piece of paper or whiteboard, such as $3x + 2 = x + 5$. Use nickels to represent the x's and the pennies to represent the single numbers. Put the corresponding number of nickels and pennies below the terms on the left side of the equation. You will need three x's (nickels) and two singles (pennies).

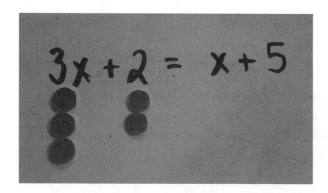

Step 2: Repeat on the right side of the equation: one x (nickel) and five singles (pennies).

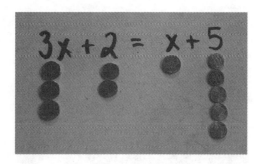

Step 3: One of the major rules of algebra is that anything you do to one side of the equation, you also do to the other. So, to simplify the equation, remove one x from both sides. The equation, shown with nickels and pennies, is now simplified to $2x + 2 = 5$.

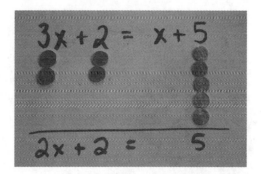

Step 4: Now remove two pennies from each side of the equals sign. You are left with two x's (nickels) equal to three singles (pennies). The equation is now simplified to $2x = 3$.

Step 5: To further simplify the equation, divide both sides by the number in front of the *x*. The number 2/2 is equal to 1, leaving just *x*. The final answer is therefore *x* = 3/2.

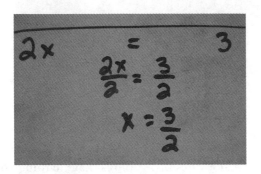

The Math Behind It

At its core, algebra is solving equations that contain letters (representing unknowns) in place of numbers. The key to solving these equations is to simplify them by doing the same thing to both sides of the equal sign. This activity reinforces that concept. Divide, multiply, subtract, or add, it doesn't really change the equation since you are doing the same thing to both sides. The coins help students realize that the letters in algebra simply take the place of something else. And in algebra, letters are used to take the place of numbers in equations.

Math for the Ages

This activity is suitable for elementary age and above. Younger students may need more guidance. Older students could do this activity while being monitored. Different-colored poker chips or large and small paper clips would also work. To solve equations that involve negative numbers or subtraction, see the next activity, Negative Poker Chips.

Negative Poker Chips

Solve one-variable equations with negative numbers using poker chips.

Algebra Concept: Simplifying one-variable algebra equations with negative terms

From the Junk Drawer:

☐ Poker chips (or bottle caps), 2 different colors

☐ Paper and pen (or whiteboard and dry-erase marker)

☐ Nickels (a third color of poker chips)

Step 1: To visualize positive and negative numbers, use a dark poker chip to represent +1 and a light poker chip to represent −1. Together, they make a zero pair. It is called a zero pair because +1 and −1 add up to 0.

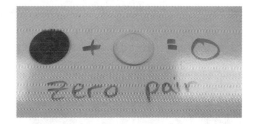

Step 2: On a piece of paper (or whiteboard), set up an example equation like $3x − 5 = 2x + 1$. Put three nickels under $3x$. (You could also use a poker chips of a different color to take the place of the x's.) Put five light-colored poker chips under −5. Subtraction is the same as adding a negative value. Repeat with two nickels and one dark chip on the other side of the equal sign.

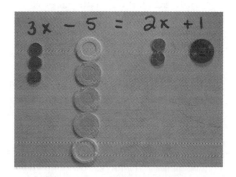

Step 3: Start by removing x's (nickels) in pairs from opposite sides of the equation until all of the x's are gone from one side. Remember, anything you do to one side of the equation, you must do to the other side. The equation is now simplified as $x - 5 = 1$

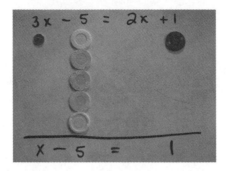

Step 4: Now, create a zero pair for each light-colored chip by adding a dark-colored chip to balance the light ones out. In the example below, that would be five dark chips. Remember, you must also add the same number of dark chips to the other side of the equal sign.

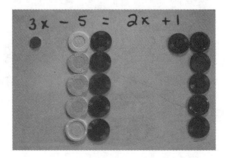

Step 5: Remove the zero pairs and you are left with the result. In this example, the equation is now simplified as $x = 6$. You have found the value of x.

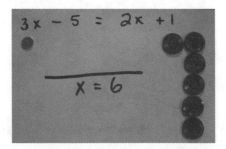

Step 6: Here is an example if you have subtraction on both sides of the equal sign. The example shown is $2x - 1 = 3x - 3$. As before, start by putting the required number of nickels and light chips under the appropriate numbers.

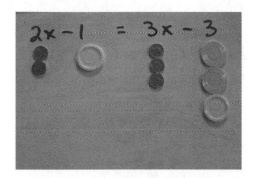

Step 7: Remove an equal number of x's (nickels) from each side until you only have x's on one side. The equation is now simplified to $-1 = x - 3$.

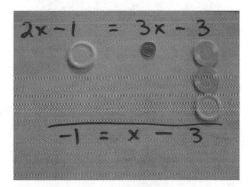

Step 8: Now, remove an equal number of light-colored chips from both sides until you have only light chips on one side of the equal sign.

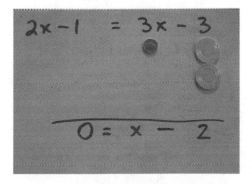

Step 9: Next, create zero pairs by adding an equal number of dark chips to cancel out the light chips. Remember, you must add the same number of chips to both sides.

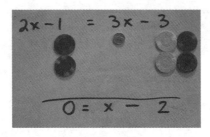

Step 10: Remove both parts of the zero pairs and you will be left with your answer: $2 = x$.

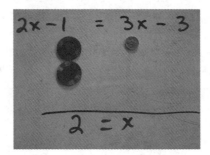

The Math Behind It

Algebra is based on using letters as variables to represent unknown numbers. Zero pairs are a great way to visualize positive and negative numbers canceling each other out. Using different-colored chips allows you to see the zero pairs and will make the algebra easier. Keep up the good work and you will master algebra in no time.

Math for the Ages

This is appropriate for all ages after negative numbers are taught. This is another great activity to reinforce that you must do the same thing to both sides of an equation in order to solve it.

Plastic Inequalities

Use colored plastic to solve for a system of inequalities.

Algebra Concepts: Inequalities, and systems of equations

From the Junk Drawer:

☐ 2 sheets of clear plastic (or 2 sheets
  of different-colored plastic)

☐ Scissors

☐ Ruler (optional)

☐ Straight-edge cutter (optional)

☐ 2 different-colored highlighters (or
  light permanent markers)

☐ Graph paper

Step 1: You will need two different-colored sheets of transparent plastic.

You can buy colored plastic wrap, but you can also make your own. (The homemade stuff works better.) Use any flat, clear plastic. The front of any plastic-wrapped, store-bought item could work. Clear plastic food containers also work well, once they have been cleaned.

Use scissors to cut the plastic into two rectangles with straight sides. A ruler is helpful to get straight edges. If you know anybody who scrapbooks, another option is to use a straight-edge cutter. The cutters are designed to trim pictures and cut perfectly straight edges.

Now use a highlighter (or light-colored permanent marker) to color the rectangle. Use a different-colored highlighter to color the other rectangle. The ink takes time to dry, so let the sheet sit for an hour to avoid the ink coming off immediately.

Step 2: Set out a piece of graph paper. Pick an inequality, such as $x > 3$. Place one of the colored plastic sheets over the grid to represent this inequality,

as shown. An inequality is an equation, but it has a greater than or less than symbol instead of (or in addition to) the equal sign.

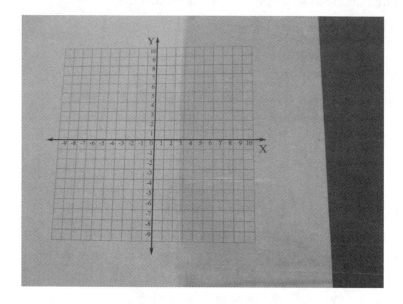

Step 3: On the same graph paper, pick another inequality, such as $y < 2$. Place the other piece of plastic on the graph to represent this inequality, as shown. In the area where both colors overlap, you have the answer to a set of inequalities. The overlap in the picture represents the numbers that solve $x > 3$ and $y < 2$.

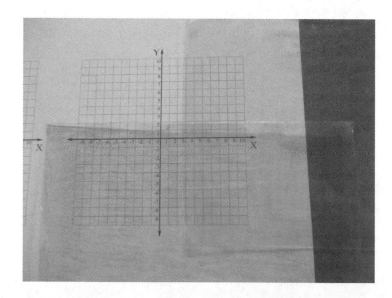

The Math Behind It

Inequalities are areas that are bounded by a function. The easiest functions to understand are equalities, which are straight lines. The formula for a straight line is $y = mx + b$. For inequalities, the signs <, >, ≤, and ≥ replace the equal sign. For the inequality $x > 3$, this is represented by the area to the right of the $x = 3$ line.

Solving systems of multiple inequalities means finding areas that overlap for two (or more) separate functions. The colored plastic makes this easy to visualize. It also saves paper as you practice, since you can use the same graph paper multiple times.

Math for the Ages

This activity is a great hands-on way to visualize a solution to a set of inequalities. This concept is usually taught later in algebra but is easy enough to understand for upper elementary students. The functions will become more complex. The colors make it very easy for teachers to walk around the room and visually check students' progress.

Curved functions can also be created, but each curve will have a slightly different shape. Each of these curves would need a new piece of plastic. An organized teacher could cut out certain shapes for curves and just use those shapes in examples, keeping the rest of the colored plastic pieces in a folder. Or, here's a better idea: have advanced students who need enrichment draw and cut the different shapes.

Powers-of-10 Cups

Use coffee cups to learn the **powers of 10**.

Algebra Concept: Powers of 10

From the Junk Drawer:

☐ 8 foam coffee cups
☐ Permanent marker

Step 1: Stack up seven coffee cups and lay them on their side. Use recycled coffee cups if they have been washed out. Write *1* on the left-hand cup top. Write a zero on each of the other six cups as shown. Then draw a line under the number to help keep the cups lined up.

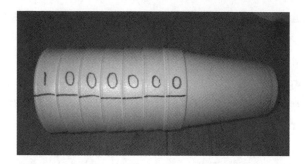

Step 2: Slide out the first cup. Write 10 to the zero power (10^0) as shown. 10 to the 0 power represents the number 1, which is what is on the cup's rim.

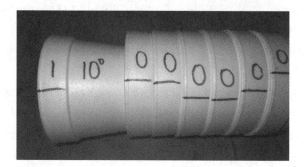

Step 3: Slide out the first cup with a zero on it. Write 10 to the first power (10^1) as shown. 10 to the first power represents the number 10. Slide the cup back in place.

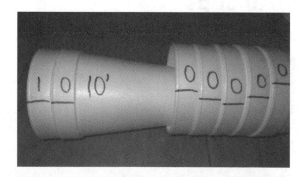

Step 4: Slide out the second cup with a *0*. Write 10 raised to the second power (10^2). This represents 100, which is what is on the cup rims. Notice the pattern: 10^2 has two *0*s.

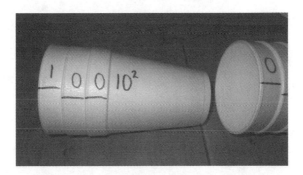

Step 5: Repeat for the remaining cups. The last cup should be 10 to the sixth power (10^6), which represents 1,000,000. It has six *0*s.

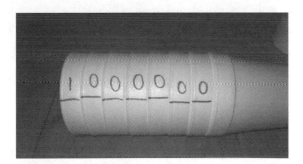

Step 6: Add an eighth blank cup to cover up the powers of 10.

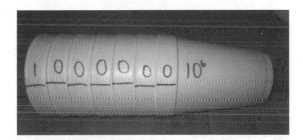

Step 7: Turn the cups over with the original numbers facing away. Draw a new line across the rims to help line the cups up. Put a big decimal point on the rim of the first cup (from the left), followed by a *1* on the second

rim. Rotate the cups up slightly and put a decimal point on the first cup's rim, followed by a *0* on the second cup's rim, followed by a *1* on the third rim. Repeat as shown until you have filled all the cups' rims.

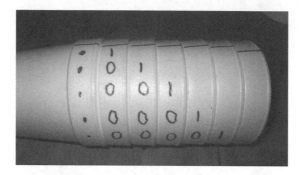

Step 8: Draw a line under the *.000001* after labeling the last cup. This will help keep the numbers lined up.

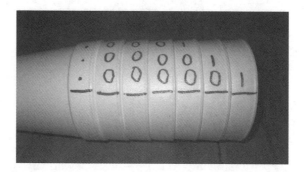

Step 9: Slide the first cup off the stack and write 10 to the −1 power (10^{-1}) on the second cup. The number .1 is equal to 10 to the −1 power.

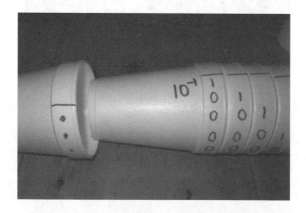

Step 10: Slide the second cup off the stack and write 10 to the −2 power (10⁻²) on the third cup. The number .01 is equal to 10 to the −2 power.

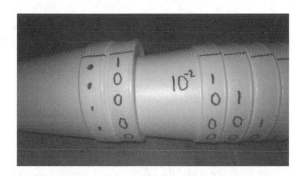

Step 11: Continue the pattern until you have 10 to the −6 power (10⁻⁶) inside the last cup. Now you have a built-in way to test if you know your powers of 10.

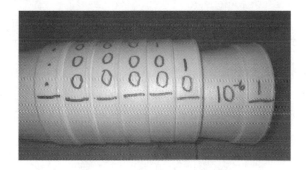

The Math Behind It

Powers of 10 are critically important in order to express very large and very small numbers, especially in **scientific notation**, which students will encounter later. The powers of 10 greater than 1 are extremely easy to understand. Ten to the first power (10^1) is a 1 followed by one 0. Ten to the second power (10^2) is a 1 followed by two 0s. This pattern continues all the way to infinity.

For numbers smaller than 1, the power exponent tells you how much smaller than 1 the number is. Ten raised to the −1 power (10^{-1}) is the same as 1 divided by 10 to the first power, or 0.1. Negative exponents always represent numbers less than 1.

Math for the Ages

Using the Power-of-10 Cups, any age can understand this concept. A larger number of cups may also be a useful teacher tool to show very large or tiny numbers. Another option is to write the prefixes for each group of three, like *kilo–*, *milli–*, and so on.

Radical Dice

Use dice in a fun activity to learn how to simplify **radicals.**

Algebra Concept: Simplifying radicals (also called square roots)

From the Junk Drawer:

☐ Paper and markers (or whiteboard and dry-erase markers)

☐ 2 dice

☐ Eraser or paper towel (optional)

Step 1: Draw a square root sign on the top of a sheet of paper (or whiteboard). When you are first learning, it is a good idea to write small enough so that you can see all the steps.

Step 2: Roll the two dice and place them under the square root sign.

Step 3: Write the digits on the dice as a two-digit number. Either digit can come first.

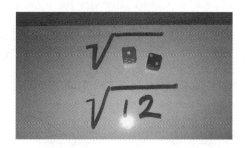

Step 4: Now simplify the number under the square root sign into simpler factors. The first step is to see if it is an even number, which would mean the number 2 is a factor. Look at the numbers that remain—can they be factored any further? (In this example, 6 can be factored again into 2 x 3.) It is OK if this takes several steps.

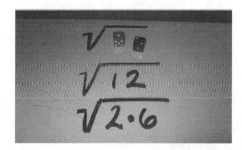

Step 5: Once you have uncovered all the factors of your original number, look for matching sets. If you have a matching set of factors, that is a perfect square. For example, if you have 2 and 2, that is a perfect square.

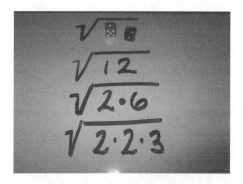

Step 6: Pull out any perfect squares in front of the square root sign. Use an eraser or paper towel to clear your whiteboard (or flip to the other side of your sheet of paper) and repeat this activity for more practice.

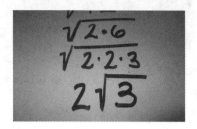

The Math Behind It

Simplifying radicals is essential to solving more complex algebra equations. This process takes practice. Perfect squares can be pulled out in front of the square root sign as a single number.

Some numbers will not simplify. For example, prime numbers only have two factors: 1 and the number itself. Prime numbers are never going to simplify, and that is OK. Others, such as the number 15, do not contain perfect squares. The only factors of 15 are 3 and 5. Just learning how to separate a number into factors is a helpful tool in algebra, even if you can't simplify the radical.

Math for the Ages

This activity is a fun way to practice factoring and to learn the concept of simplifying radicals. The use of whiteboards is also an easier way to practice this skill, and its saves paper. For more than one student, the dice could be rolled where everybody sees them and then you can have a race to the finish. Stores sell large foam dice that would be perfect for a classroom setting. Having the students rotate getting out of their seats to roll the dice is a good way to get the students moving a little. Anytime you add something to math besides paper and pencil, you grab students' attention.

It is possible to buy eight- or ten-sided dice for larger numbers. (On a 10-sided die, the 10 will be a 0 for this activity.) You could also use a deck of cards. If you use cards, eliminate the face cards. Just deal two cards to create the number under the square root sign.

Tasty Factoring

Use cereal to help students learn factoring.

Algebra Concept: Factoring

From the Junk Drawer:

☐ 24 pieces (or more) of cereal (or pennies, dried beans, or poker chips)

Step 1: Create a 4-by-6 rectangle out of the cereal pieces as shown. The rectangle has 24 total pieces. Given its dimensions, 4 and 6 are both factors of 24.

Step 2: Create a 2-by-12 rectangle out of the cereal pieces. It also has 24 total pieces, and the factors are now 2 and 12.

Step 3: Create a 3-by-8 rectangle out of the cereal pieces. You still have 24 total pieces, and the factors are now 3 and 8.

Step 4 You can also rotate your rectangles to show the factors of 24 in a different order. Create a tall 8-by-3 rectangle out of the cereal pieces. The rectangle still has 24 total pieces, and 8 and 3 are still the factors.

The Math Behind It

Factors are one of the most important basic elements of algebra. Factoring involves splitting numbers (or equations) into the components that, when multiplied, give you the original value. Since multiplication is commutative, it doesn't matter what order they are multiplied in. Knowing how to factor a number makes simplification easy.

Factoring is easiest to see at first using actual numbers, not unknowns or variables. But factoring still works with more complex algebraic terms. For example, $3x$ has factors of 3 and x. And x squared (x^2) has factors of x and x. You will even encounter numbers that have more than two factors. For example, 24 factors into 2, 3, and 4. When you multiply $2 \times 3 \times 4$, you get 24. Taken even further, 24 factors into 2, 3, 2, and 2 (because 4 is 2×2). Written out, $2 \times 3 \times 2 \times 2 = 24$.

Math for the Ages

This activity is a great way to introduce factoring and is suitable for students of any age, as long as they have some experience with multiplication. It is even a great way to introduce multiplication to the younger crowd.

Thumbtack Graph Paper

Turn scrap cardboard and string into reusable graph paper.

Algebra Concept: Graphing straight lines from coordinate points

Adult supervision required

From the Junk Drawer:

☐ 1 square of corrugated cardboard (at
   least 1 foot by 1 foot)

☐ Scissors

☐ Ruler

☐ Permanent marker

☐ Thumbtacks (or pushpins)

☐ String or yarn

Step 1: With an adult's help, cut out a square of corrugated cardboard. You
will be using a ruler and a permanent marker to create a 10-inch-by-10-
inch square of graph paper on the cardboard. Start by drawing the y-axis
and marking every inch.

Step 2: Draw the x-axis and mark every inch.

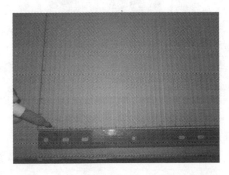

Step 3: To keep the lines straight, use a dot to mark every inch going up on the side opposite your *y*-axis.

Step 4: Use a ruler and a marker to draw horizontal lines.

Step 5: Now use a ruler and marker to draw vertical lines. Label each line, starting with *0* in the lower left corner.

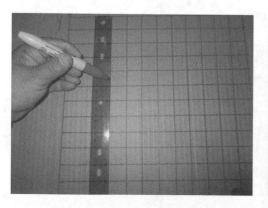
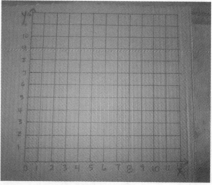

Step 6: Place a thumbtack at (2,4). This is called an ordered pair and is represented by (*x*-coordinate, *y*-coordinate). To find its location, move two to the right on the *x*-axis and up four on the *y*-axis.

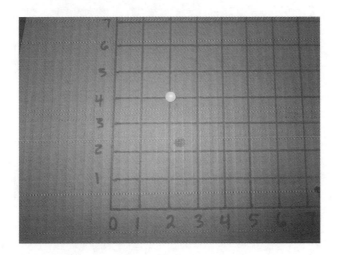

Step 7: Put another thumbtack at some other intersection point on the grid. Stretch a piece of string and tack it down using the thumbtacks. (With thick string that has been wound in a ball, you may want to add additional thumbtacks to keep the line straight. Thin string can be wrapped around the post of the pin, under the head.)

You can now calculate the equation for the line. The general equation is $y = mx + b$. The letter *m* is used to stand for the slope (which is the rise/run). And *b* is the *y* intercept, where the line intersects the *y*-axis.

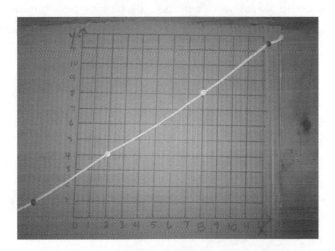

Step 8: You can create a new line and reinforce the concept of y-intercept by moving both thumbtacks down two spaces on the y-axis. The line will have the same slope (m), but a new y-intercept.

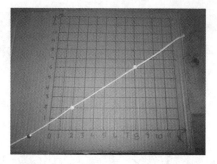

Step 9: You can also demonstrate a rough parabola by using a thumbtack to secure the top of each end of the string and letting it hang down. Thin string (or yarn) will probably give you a smoother shape.

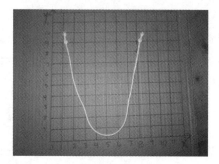

Step 10: You could also show a hyperbola by placing one thumbtack high on the left, near the y-axis, and another thumbtack low and to the right, near the x-axis.

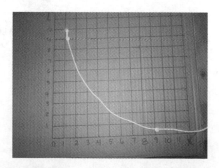

The Math Behind It

Graphing is fundamental to algebra. Thumbtack Graph Paper is a great reusable way to practice graphing. Straight lines, parabolas, hyperbolas, and intersecting lines can all be created with this activity.

Math for the Ages

Graphing is usually taught in middle school but can be understood earlier by bright students. Making the Thumbtack Graph Paper can be a fun activity. Pushpins are safer and easier to manipulate, but thumbtacks work just as well. For teachers, hang on to these creations and reuse them for a few years.

Transitive Sticky Notes

Use sticky notes to learn the **transitive property**.

Algebra Concept: Transitive property

From the Junk Drawer:

☐ Sticky notes (or index cards)   ☐ Marker

Step 1: Write A, B, and an equal sign on three different sticky notes. Align them so they say $A = B$.

Step 2: Write B, C, and an equal sign on three more sticky notes. Align them so they say $B = C$. Put them to the right of the $A = B$ notes.

Step 3: Because $B = B$, remove the Bs and one of the equals signs. The resulting equation shows you that $A = C$. This is the definition of the transitive property. Of course, you can move the A and C closer together to make it easier to see.

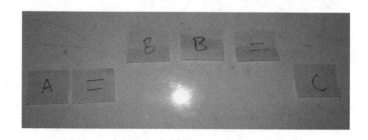

The Math Behind It

The full name for this algebraic property is the transitive property of equalities. A fellow teacher calls it the "eliminating the middleman" property. If $A = B$ and $B = C$, then by the transitive property, A must equal C.

The transitive property also works for inequalities as long as the inequality signs point in the same direction. For example, if $A > B$ and $B > C$, then by the transitive property, $A > C$.

Math for the Ages

This activity is appropriate for all ages. It is a great way to introduce mathematical properties. Using sticky notes is a great way to visualize the concept for students.

3

Algebra Labs

When you *do* something, you will learn it better. To learn to skate, put skates on. To ride a bike, you have to get on a bicycle. The same is true for math. Algebra labs are a great way to learn math. Time to get your hands dirty!

Bouncing Balls

Use a bouncy ball, a yardstick, and a smartphone to create an exponential function.

Algebra Concept: **Exponential decay functions**

From the Junk Drawer:

☐ Yardstick or meter stick
☐ Wall
☐ Tape (optional)
☐ Helper
☐ Smartphone

☐ Tripod (optional)
☐ Bouncy ball
☐ Graph paper
☐ Pen or pencil

Step 1: Stand a yardstick (or meter stick) up against a wall with a hard-surface floor, like tile, concrete, or hardwood. You might want to add a piece of tape to hold the yardstick in place. (Get permission from an adult

before you use tape on a wall.) Painter's tape is a great choice, because it
never damages paint.

Position a friend with a smartphone (or video camera) set to record
video. It is important that the phone is level down near the bottom of the
yardstick. You also need to be able to clearly see the entire yardstick in the
frame of the video. A tripod can serve as a phone support, if you have one
handy.

Line up the bottom of the bouncy ball with the top of the yardstick.
Press record on the video and then drop the ball. Stop the video once the
ball stops bouncing. It is easy to repeat it if you want a better video. This
can also be done without the video, if you have a friend squat down and
see where the bottom of the ball is after each bounce.

Since you are always dropping from the same height, you can repeat as
many times as needed to get all of your data.

Step 2: Make a data table for your measurements like the one shown at the
top of the next page. Now watch the video. The ball was dropped from
36 inches (or 100 centimeters) to start, so record that distance for bounce
0. Observe the video to see how high the ball rises after the first bounce,
measured at the bottom of the ball. Most video players have a slow-motion
feature to make this easier to see. Record the height in the data table.

View the next bounce and record the height for bounce 2 in the data table. Repeat until you can no longer see how high the ball bounces.

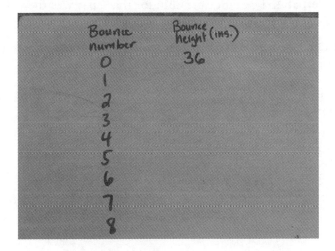

Step 3: Graph your data on graph paper (or a whiteboard). The bounce number goes on the x-axis and the bounce height goes on the y-axis. The graph that you create is an example of an exponential decay function.

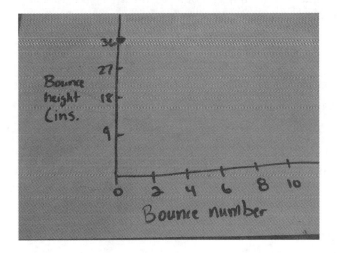

The Math Behind It

Exponential decays are a common math graph shape found in nature. Naturally radioactive elements, sales of consumer fads, and even voting trends are a few things that are studied using exponential decay functions. The formula $y = a(1 - b)^x$ is the generic exponential decay formula. The variable y equals how much is left after a certain time unit; for this lab, y was the bounce height. The letter a represents how much you start with; for this lab, a was 36 inches (or 100 centimeters). The letter b represents the percent change for each bounce. For this lab, this would depend on what type of ball you used. Rubber balls are going to bounce higher each time compared to a Ping-Pong ball. The variable x represents time; for this lab, x was the bounce number.

You can try different balls, different surfaces, and different initial drop heights to plot more curves like this. But it is important in any lab to change only one variable at a time. As you alter one variable and compare data, you will see a pattern emerge. The shapes of all the graphs will be the same, but how steep the curve is will change.

Math for the Ages

This is a great activity to introduce exponential decay functions, which are commonly taught at the high school level. But this lab is doable for almost any age with a little help. It makes a great way to front-load the brain of a precocious child.

For teachers or homeschool teachers of older students, this activity can be modified to introduce natural logs and do the math with the equation above. Depending on the equipment you have, you can tweak the activity in a few ways. In my classroom, we use microphones to record the times between bounces. You can use one half of the time between bounces, because that is how much time it takes the ball to reach the top of the bounce each time. Using the equation $h = \frac{1}{2}gt^2$ (where h = height, g = acceleration of gravity, and t = time), you can solve for height since the acceleration of gravity is a constant. You can also calculate the half-life of the bouncing ball by estimating the number of bounces it would take for the ball to get to half of the original drop height.

Buying School Supplies

"Buy" junk drawer supplies to learn equations.

Algebra Concept: Simple algebraic equations

From the Junk Drawer:

☐ Sticky notes

☐ Marker

☐ Random desk supplies, several of each (paper clips, pens, erasers, etc.)

Step 1: Use sticky notes to price various desk supplies with prices of 5¢, 10¢, 25¢, etc.

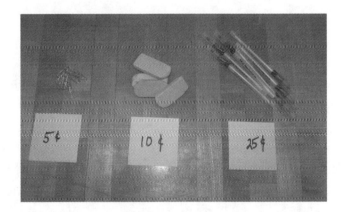

Step 2: Let students pick two types of supplies to reach $1. They can choose as many of each type as they want. For example, five paper clips (5¢ each) and three pens (25¢ each) would equal 100¢, or $1.00.

Step 3: Now, write an equation with sticky notes that matches what the student "purchased." For this example, $5c + 3p = 1.00$ where $c = .05$ and $p = .25$. This teaches students the meaning of equations and gives them a visual cue.

The Math Behind It

Equations are a guide to thinking. Money is almost always understood by all levels of students after early elementary ages. Combining the two can help teach the importance of coefficients and constants. The c and the p in the example problem are constants, which represent the cost of each school supply. The coefficients represent the number of each school supply students buy. In future algebra classes, students may be given the coefficients and asked to solve for the constant values.

Math for the Ages

This activity is suitable for elementary age and above. It could serve as a valuable way to introduce algebraic equations. This could also be done with cereal pieces for a larger class.

A Car Is Really Heavy

Weigh your car using simple junk drawer tools and the power of math.

Algebra Concept: Three-variable algebra

Adult supervision required

From the Junk Drawer:

☐ Paper and pencil

☐ Car

☐ Ruler (marked in inches)

☐ Tire pressure gauge

☐ Calculator (optional)

☐ Computer with Internet connection
 (optional)

Step 1: Create a table as shown to record your data.

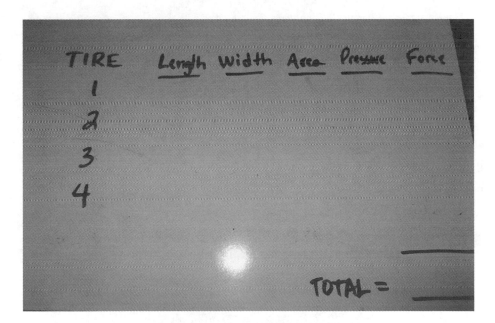

Step 2: Look at one of the tires of the car you want to weigh. What shape
does the bottom of the tire make with the ground? It makes a rectangle,
or at least very close to a rectangle. For this activity, you will first measure
the length of the rubber in contact with the ground—you will have to get

down on your knees to accurately measure this. Measure to the nearest ¼ inch. Record the length data in your table.

Step 3: Next, measure the width of the rubber in contact with the ground. You need to reach under the tire to feel that the back of the ruler is even with the back edge of the tire. Measure the width of the tire to the nearest ¼ inch. Record the width data in your table.

Step 4: With an adult's help, remove the cap on the tire's air nozzle. Use the tire pressure gauge to read the air pressure inside the tire. Record the pressure data in your table.

Step 5: Calculate the area of the tire. The area of the tire in contact with the ground is length times width. You can use a calculator or do it by hand. The area will have units of square inches. Record the area you calculated in your table.

Pressure is equal to force divided by area. By doing simple algebra, you can see that force is equal to pressure times area. So the force is the weight (in pounds) on that individual tire.

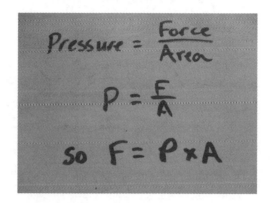

$$Pressure = \frac{Force}{Area}$$

$$P = \frac{F}{A}$$

$$So \quad F = P \times A$$

Step 6: Repeat Steps 2 through 5 for each tire until the data table is complete. Since the only things touching the ground are the four tires, you can add the four weights together to get the total weight of the car. (Your value will be too high, but we will get to that shortly.)

Step 7: Open the driver's door and look for a white sticker. On that sticker will be a line that reads "Gross Vehicle Weight." This is the empty weight of your car; the actual weight will be within 100 pounds of this number, because of gas, items in the trunk, etc.

If your car does not have the white sticker, you will have to get permission or help from an adult to use the Internet. No sticker probably means the car was in an accident at some point. Put the year and model of car followed by "gross vehicle weight" into a search engine, and you should be able to find it. Your calculated number will be higher than the actual weight, but there is a valid reason for that. Look at the part of the tire in the air. What do you see? Do you see any pattern in the rubber? Keep thinking about how that pattern would change any of the values you calculated. The explanation is below if you are still stumped.

The Math Behind It

Your car rests on four tires. The entire weight of the car goes through only those four patches of rubber. Pressure equals force divided by area, so force (weight) is equal to pressure times area. The weight you calculated is high because of the tire treads.

If you look at the tire, you see tread. The grooves in the tread are not actually touching the ground. Only the lowest black rubber parts are touching the ground. This means the area you calculated is too large. It would be very difficult to measure just the black rubber actually touching the ground. Since your area is too large, the calculated weight is too large. Only about 50 percent of the area you calculated is rubber hitting the road.

Most people erroneously think tread is for friction. But tread is there to get water and mud out from under the tire. Look at drag race car tires, they have no tread because they need maximum friction. NASCAR and Formula 1 racing is also done without tread. If you do the same experiment with a race car, your calculated weight would be much closer to the car's actual weight.

Your number will also be slightly off because the area is not a perfect rectangle. But it is amazing that air is holding your car off the ground. Air pressure can be really powerful. Weighing your car is a great way to learn some of the beauty of math.

Math for the Ages

Preschoolers and young elementary age students can understand the simple idea of air pressure, but this activity is probably too advanced for most. Upper elementary age and middle school students can handle this with a little structure and guidance. For high school, this is a great inquiry lab. Just give the students the formula and the tools, and turn them loose.

Decaying Candy

Use candy to understand exponential decay of atoms.

Algebra Concept: Decay functions

From the Junk Drawer:

- ☐ Paper and pen (or whiteboard and dry-erase marker)
- ☐ M&Ms or other double-sided candies with a letter on one side
- ☐ Clean cup (or small plastic container)
- ☐ Clean paper plate (or towel)
- ☐ Plastic sandwich bag (optional)
- ☐ Graph paper

Step 1: Make a table for your data as shown. Count the total number of candies in your sample and put them in a clean cup. Write that number down by the "0 shakes" mark in your data table.

Step 2: Shake the cup and pour the candy out on a clean paper plate. You might need to smooth them out to get them all to lay flat on the plate. Discard (or eat) the candies that have the *M* facing up. The *M* represents candies that have decayed or changed. Record the number of "good" (*M* down) candies left.

Step 3: Pour the remaining candies back into the cup. Repeat Step 2. After each shake, remove the candies with the *M* facing up and record the number left in your data chart. If you have eaten enough, put the "decayed" candies in a plastic sandwich bag and save them for later.

Step 4: Repeat Steps 2 and 3 until all of the candies have "decayed."

Step 5: Graph the data to see a decay function. Put the number of good atoms (candies) up the side (*y*-axis) and the number of shakes across the bottom of the graph (*x*-axis). Draw a smooth curve through the data points. This is called the line of best fit. The shape you will see is not a straight line but a curve. This specific shape is called an exponential decay function.

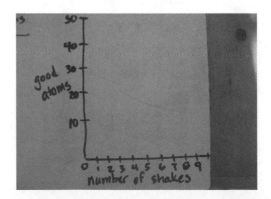

The Math Behind It

Exponential decay functions occur in the real world in many areas. The natural decay of radioactive elements is probably the most common example. Radio-active decay functions for elements are used to measure the age of old material that was once alive, like fossils. This is one of many examples that shows that science and math go together in so many ways.

Radioactive dating for dinosaur fossils is used to date the rock the fossils were found inside. In this activity, you shook the cup to cause the candies to "decay," as shown by the number of pieces where the M flipped up. In nature, some elements will naturally decay. But the time it takes the elements to decay varies. This time is called the half-life of an element. The half-life is the time it takes for half of a substance to decay into something new. By studying how much of a certain element is left in the rock, scientists can get a number for the age of the rock.

Scientists use the same shape graph you created, but they have years across the bottom instead of shakes. For potassium-40, each shake would be the same as 1.25 billion years. That means scientists can determine the age of rocks back 7 or 8 billion years! If they determine how old the rock is, they know how long ago the dinosaur lived.

Math for the Ages

This activity is suitable for all ages, but younger groups will need some adult help. Seeing the shape is valuable. This lab can also be done with coins, where heads up would represent the M up, if you don't want to feed the kids candy. For middle and high school grades, you could add the concept of half-life, which is a science/math concept used with decay functions.

Doubling Cereal

Learn the power of doubling with cereal.

Algebra Concepts: Doubling, and powers of 2

From the Junk Drawer:

☐ Cereal (or rice)   ☐ Clock or stopwatch

☐ Paper towel   ☐ Paper and pen (optional)

Step 1: Place a single piece of cereal on a paper towel (so you can eat it later). You could also do this with grains of rice. For a large classroom, a single bag of rice would probably be enough for everybody.

Step 2: Pick a doubling time, one minute works well. Set up a clock or stopwatch where you can see it—you will double the pieces of cereal every minute. You might want to make a table on paper to record your values.

Step 3: After a minute has passed, add an equal number of pieces (one piece) to the paper towel.

Step 4: After another minute, add two more pieces of cereal. Continue to double the number of pieces each minute.

Step 5: Repeat for 10 minutes or until you get tired. To keep the pattern up, double 8 to get 16, etc. You might even run out of cereal.

The Math Behind It

Doubling what you have allows the numbers to grow rapidly. What you are actually using is the powers of 2. In Step 1, 2 raised to the 0 power (2^0) is 1. Next, 2 raised to the first power (2^1) is 2. Then, 2 raised to the second power (2^2) is 4; 2 raised to the third power (2^3) is 8. The number gets large fast.

Math Through the Ages

This is age appropriate for almost all classrooms to show the power of doubling. Raising 2 to various powers is best suited for upper elementary and beyond. This activity would also be a great way to introduce the "y to the x" button on a scientific calculator. Put the number 2 in your calculator and then hit the "y^x" button. Push the 5 button and you will be raising 2 to the fifth power (2^5). The answer will be 32—you have doubled the number 2 five times.

Falling for You

Use two smartphones to create a perfect parabola.

Algebra Concept: Parabola

From the Junk Drawer:

- ☐ Clear tape
- ☐ Tape measure (or meter stick)
- ☐ 1 board (about 3 feet long)
- ☐ Several books (or 1 plastic container)
- ☐ 2 smartphones
- ☐ Ball
- ☐ Paper and pen
- ☐ Graph paper

Step 1: Use clear tape to attach a tape measure (or meter stick) to a board. Stack a few books or a plastic container (about the size of a shoebox) under one end of the board. Set one smartphone to the stopwatch feature.

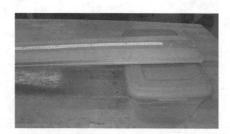

Step 2: The second smartphone will be used to record a video of the ball rolling down the ramp and the time count on the first phone.

When ready, with the video rolling on the second phone, release the ball to roll down the ramp.

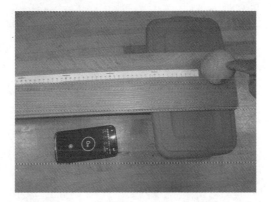

Step 3: Look at the recording and you will see the distance rolled each second. Use the front edge of the ball as your measuring point. Record the distance traveled each second in a data chart. Then make a graph of distance versus time. It will look like a parabola.

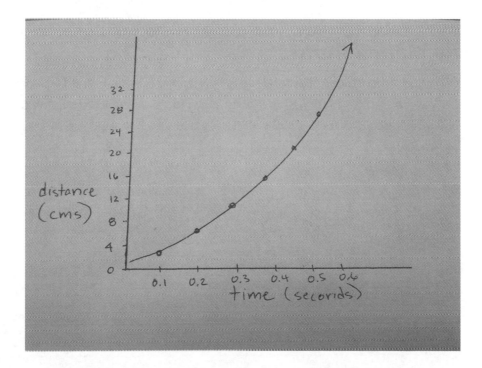

Step 4: You can repeat the experiment, raising the ramp to a greater angle, to get a steeper parabola. You can even stand the board vertically and drop the ball if you have a good video recorder on your phone.

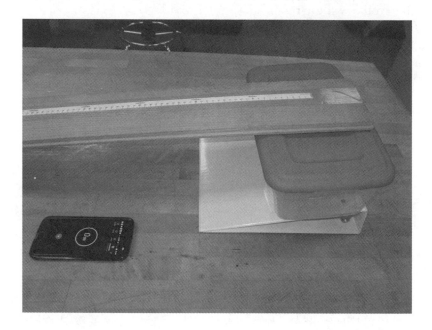

The Math Behind It

Galileo first did this experiment to look at accelerated motion in the 1600s. He didn't have the fancy timers we have today. He used pendulums to keep time. A ball rolling down an incline will produce a parabola when time versus distance is graphed.

Using geometry, Galileo developed one of the first methods to accurately determine the acceleration due to gravity. The stopwatches and video recorders we have today allow us to do the same experiment that Galileo worked on for over a month. You can do it in a few minutes.

Math for the Ages

This activity is suitable for lower elementary-age students and up to create the shape of a parabola. Younger students may need some help to use the smartphones.

Folded Paper

Learn about exponential functions by folding paper.

Algebra Concept: Exponential growth

From the Junk Drawer:

☐ 1 full-size sheet of paper ☐ Paper or whiteboard

☐ Pen ☐ Graph paper (optional)

☐ Ruler

Step 1: Start with a normal full-size sheet of paper. This could be done with gently used paper from your recycling bin. Fold the paper in half and crease the edge. Now unfold it and count the number of sections. (A pen was used to darken the fold line for the photograph below; you can use a ruler to darken yours as well, if you desire.)

Make a table to record your results for the next few steps. In the first column, write the number of folds, and in the second column, record the number of sections. In this step, one fold creates two sections. (Refold the paper after counting the sections.)

Step 2: Fold the paper again. Then unfold it and count the number of sections. You now have two folds and four sections. Write this information down in your table. Refold the paper for the next step.

Step 3: Fold the paper a third time. Unfold and count the number of sections. You now have three folds and eight sections. Write it down in your table. Refold the paper for the next step.

Step 4: Fold the paper a fourth time. Unfold it and count: four folds and 16 sections. Write this down in your table. Refold the paper.

Step 5: Fold the paper once more. Unfold and count the number of sections. You now have five folds and 32 sections. Write it down in your table and refold the paper.

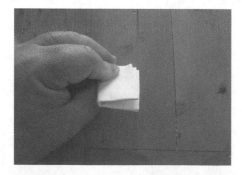

Step 6: If you can, fold the paper again. This is difficult because of the thickness of the paper now. Unfold and count the number of sections. You now have six folds and 64 sections. The folds will not be super sharp now, so you might want to use a pen to darken the fold lines to make it easier to count, as in the photo. Write the number of folds and sections down in your table.

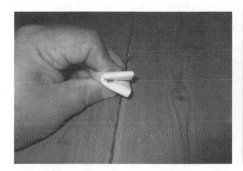 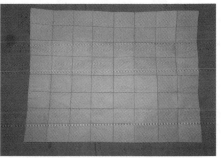

Step 7: Now create a graph with the number of sections on the *y*-axis and the number of folds on the *x*-axis as shown. The graph could be done on graph paper to make it easier. Plot the points from your table on the graph. Draw a smooth curve through all the points. This graph represents exponential growth.

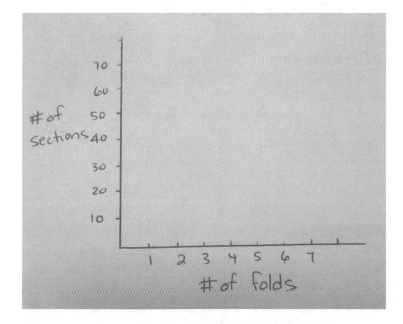

The Math Behind It

The curve you created is an example of exponential growth. Your function would be $y = 2^x$, where y is the number of sections and x is the number of folds. So when there is one fold, you have 2 raised to the first power, which is 2 ($2^1 = 2$). When you have three folds, you have 2 raised to the third power, which is 8 ($2^3 = 8$).

Many things in real life exhibit exponential growth for a period of time, but they reach a physical limit after some time. For example, if you could (you can't, by the way) continue folding the paper 14 times, it would be taller than your head!

Math for the Ages

This activity is appropriate for all ages. Younger children will struggle getting past four or five folds, but that is OK. They will still see the shape of the graphs.

Math Is in the Cards

Play cards to learn **mean**, median, **mode**, and **range**.

Algebra Concepts: Mean, median, mode, range

From the Junk Drawer:

☐ Deck of cards (jokers removed)   ☐ Calculator

Step 1: Randomly pick seven cards from a standard deck. Face cards all count as 10 and aces count as 1. Lay the cards out from smallest to largest value. You could really do this with any number of cards, but seven is a good starting point.

Step 2: First, calculate the mean of the numbers (commonly called the *average*). Do this by adding all the numbers up and dividing by seven, since you have seven cards. Round off the number to two places after the decimal point, just to keep the number looking manageable.

Step 3: Next, find the median, which is the middle of your values. Start by flipping over the outside end cards.

Step 4: Continue flipping over each set of outside cards until you just have a single card left in the middle. This card is the median of your values. If you have an even number of cards, you will be left with two cards face up and the average of those two will be the median.

Step 5: Next, find the mode. Turn all the cards back face up. The mode is the most commonly found value. Slide up any cards that have the same value. It is possible to have two or more modes.

Step 6: The last statistic to examine is the range. The range is defined by the outside cards. The lowest value is the bottom of the range and the highest value is the top of the range.

The Math Behind It

Statistics is an interesting math topic. Statistics helps provide the tools for studying measured values. And if you study those measured values enough, you can apply algebra to the measurements to create algebraic equations.

Studying numbers is essential in some jobs, like teaching, insurance, medical research, and more. The most common statistical values are the four terms you just learned about. Mean is usually called the average, and is likely the term you are most familiar with. The median is an important statistical number because it tells you the middle value in a set of numbers. If a class full of students takes a test, the mean could be very high because of a few very high scores. But sometimes the median gives a teacher a better overall sense of how the class did. The mode and range are easy to understand and can be very useful in evaluating student performance.

Math for the Ages

This activity is suitable for all ages. Even the youngest student can use this as a beginning to understanding statistics. For older students, a few decks of cards can help an entire class visualize the concepts. Some will get numbers easily, but some need and appreciate the hands-on aspect of this activity.

Paper River

Use cheap wrapping paper and a toy to find out how to canoe across a fast river.

Algebra Concept: Adding speeds with the **Pythagorean theorem**

From the Junk Drawer:

□ Long piece of wrapping paper
□ Meter stick
□ Battery-operated toy car
□ Helper

□ Smartphone or calculator and stopwatch
□ Paper and pen
□ Tape

Step 1: Turn a sheet of wrapping paper blank side up. Use a meter stick to measure the distance across the paper "river." Then turn on a battery-operated toy car and drive it across the paper while your helper uses a smartphone's stopwatch to time how long the car takes to cross the river. Repeat at least three times to get an average time.

Use a calculator (also on the smartphone) to calculate the car's average speed. This is found by taking distance divided by the average time. Write down the car's speed on a sheet of paper. The car will represent a boat.

Step 2: With the car on the paper, have a friend practice pulling the paper beneath it at a constant speed. This moving paper is the flowing river. Measure the distance your friend moved the paper and the time it took to cover that distance. Calculate the river speed by dividing distance by time. Write down the river's speed on a sheet of paper.

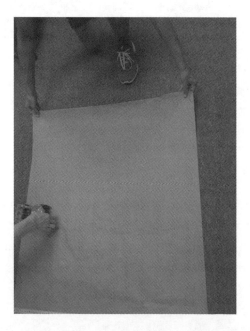

Step 3: Now place the car on the "river" perpendicular to the "shore." Pull the paper at the same speed it was pulled before, but let the car drive across the paper as it is pulled. It may take a little practice to get good at it. You also may want to put a piece of tape on the floor next to the river to mark the starting point.

Step 4: Place another piece of tape where the "boat" reaches the other side of the "river." You can also use a smartphone to record the river trip from above, but you will need to lay a meter stick down to get the starting and finishing points.

Step 5: Looking at the starting and ending points, you'll notice the boat's path was actually along the **hypotenuse** of the triangle formed by the river speed (the paper) and the boat speed (the car). The boat's total speed is greater than the speed the boat actually moved!

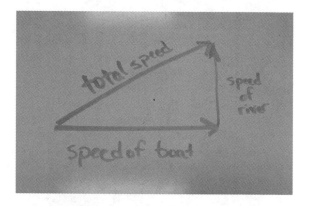

Step 6: Now try to get the boat to go straight across the river. You will need to aim the boat up the river, angled like the hypotenuse in reverse, to accomplish this feat. This takes practice. This is what kayakers and canoeists do to go straight across a river.

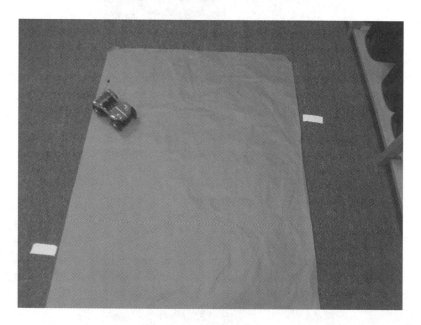

The Math Behind It

I've used this lab in my physics class for years. But if you watch how the car is pulled with the river, it is a math problem. The river's speed and the boat's speed are perpendicular to each other. The Pythagorean theorem will allow you to solve for the actual speed of the "boat," which is a combination of the speed vector of the river and the speed vector of the boat. You can also experiment with changing the angle of the boat until the boat goes straight across the paper river.

If you live near a river that is popular with kayakers or canoeists, you can see this activity in action. The kayakers paddle at an angle into the river to go straight across. They are actually paddling along an imaginary hypotenuse created by the kayaker's speed and the water speed.

Math for the Ages

This is a great hands-on activity for exploring the Pythagorean theorem. It is doable for elementary age and above. You can also use the same concept for positive and negative numbers if you go with the river or against the river (in the same direction as the water), instead of across the river (perpendicular). Moving with the river, you add the river speed and boat speed to get the total speed. Going against the river, you add the boat speed and the negative river speed to get the total speed.

This might seem like a geometry lab, but Common Core algebra standards want students to understand equations that describe relationships. This well-known equation is a great way to reinforce that equations show relationships. Each individual part of the motion—the river and the boat—is a vector. Vectors are used in linear algebra, which is usually included in Algebra 2.

For teachers, bulletin board paper works perfectly as a substitute for the wrapping paper. It can be rolled up and reused, or you can just use it when you change your bulletin board. In my class, the students do all their calculations and draw the boat's path on the paper. Then I hang it up for other students to see.

Pi-endulum

Use string to determine pi and keep time.

Algebra Concept: Simplifying and solving an algebraic equation

From the Junk Drawer:

☐ Weight

☐ String

☐ Tape (optional)

☐ Smartphone or stopwatch

☐ Ruler

Step 1: Tie a weight to the end of a piece of string. A binder clip, pen, key ring, or almost anything will work, as long as it has a bit of weight. Tie (or tape) the other end of the string to a tabletop or desktop. The Pi-endulum should swing freely.

Step 2: Pull the weight back at angle and let it swing freely. The angle doesn't matter as long as the weight doesn't hit anything. Let it swing freely and use a smartphone stopwatch to time five complete swings. A complete swing includes the complete back and forth vibration. To get the time for one swing, you will divide by five. This time represents the period of your Pi-endulum and is T in the equation you will solve.

Step 3: Accurately measure the length of the Pi-endulum from the top pivot to the middle of your weight in centimeters. Divide this value by 100 to convert centimeters into meters. This represents length (*l*) in the equation.

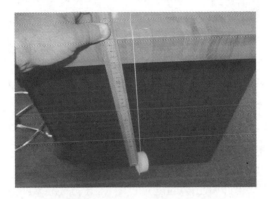

Step 4: The period of a pendulum is given by the formula T = 2π × √(length/acceleration of gravity). Using algebra, solve the following equation for *g*, the acceleration due to gravity. This will take some practice to get right.

First, square both sides of the equation to "remove" the square root:
$T^2 = (2\pi \times \sqrt{(l/g)})^2$
which becomes:
$T^2 = 4\pi^2 \times l/g$
Multiply both sides of the equation by *g*:
$g \times T^2 = g \times 4\pi^2 \times l/g$
which, when simplified, becomes:
$g \times T^2 = 4\pi^2 \times l$
Divide each side by T^2 to make:
$g \times T^2 / T^2 = 4\pi^2 \times l / T^2$
which, when simplified, becomes:
$g = 4\pi^2 \times l/T^2$
The value for *g* should be close to 9.8 meters/second².

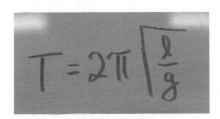

The Math Behind It

Pendulums have been used to measure time for centuries. Most clocks today keep time using electricity, but pendulums will still do the job. Grandfather clocks and cuckoo clocks are common clocks that still are powered by pendulums.

The time for one complete swing of a pendulum is called the period (T). The period of a pendulum depends only on the length of the pendulum and the acceleration of gravity. The acceleration of gravity depends on your elevation but is very close to 9.8 meters per second squared at most places where people live. (It is slightly lower at the top of Mount Everest.) There are free smartphone apps that will allow you to see the acceleration of gravity at your location.

Playground swings are examples of life-size pendulums. You could even do this activity outside with a swing set if you wanted to. The weight doesn't affect the period of the pendulum, and it would be easy to see that using a swing. You also could try different weights indoors, but make sure you keep the length of the string constant.

Math for the Ages

This activity is a great way to combine math and science. Solving the equation for g is probably best left to middle school and above. Another option is to vary the length of the pendulum, then graph the length on the x-axis and the period on the y-axis. This will result in a square root curve. This may be a new shape for many people. A square root curve shows that the period varies with the square root of length. The acceleration of gravity is fairly constant in a particular location.

Probability Cards

Learn the basics of probability with playing cards.
Algebra Concepts: Number sense, probability

From the Junk Drawer:

☐ Full deck of playing cards (jokers removed)
☐ Paper and pen (or whiteboard and dry-erase marker)

Step 1: You have to know a few facts about your cards. A normal deck contains 13 cards in each of 4 suits, for 52 cards total. You therefore have four of each individual card—four jacks, or four 2s, etc.

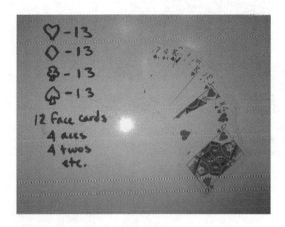

Step 2: The probability of getting anything is the possible number of successes divided by the number to choose from.

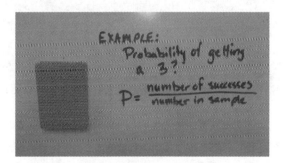

Step 3: So the probability of drawing a 3 is 4/52. There are four cards with the number 3 and 52 possible choices.

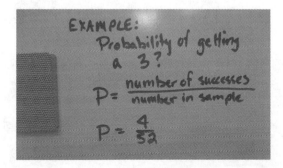

Step 4: Try a few. What is the probability of getting a diamond? (Answer below in The Math Behind It)

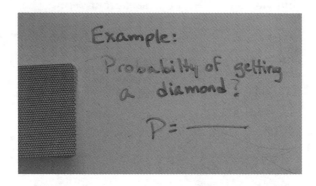

Step 5: What is the probability of getting a 10 of spades? (Answer below in The Math Behind It)

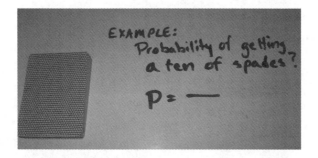

Step 6: Probability for *two* events happening is more complicated but understandable. For example, what is the probability of drawing two number 5 cards? First, calculate the probability of drawing a single 5, which is 4/52.

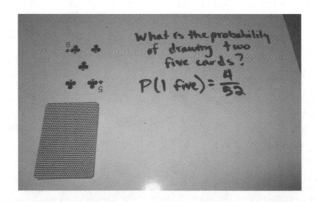

Step 7: Now, you are going to multiply that probability by the probability of drawing a second 5.

Step 8: The probability of drawing a second 5 is 3 (since there are only three 5s left) divided by 51 (since there are only 51 cards left to choose from).

Step 9: When you multiply the two probability values together, you get the probability of drawing two number 5 cards.

The Math Behind It

Probability is the chance of anything happening. A more common phrase is to call it the odds that something will happen. Probability is the reason it is so hard to win the lottery. In simple terms, the probability (odds) are heavily against you winning it. Probability is taught in middle school and then expanded upon in high school algebra (usually in Algebra 2).

Answers to Steps 4 and 5: probability of getting a diamond: 13/52 (or reduced, ¼); probability of getting a 10 of spades: 1/52.

Math for the Ages

This activity is suitable for all ages, with the exception of the two-card calculation. The math for that is best left to middle elementary grades and beyond. Preschoolers may want to start with coin flipping. For that, your probability of flipping a heads is one out of two.

Sidewalk Chalk Math

Combine chemistry and math to determine the number of chalk molecules you use when you write your name on the sidewalk.

Algebra Concepts: Scientific notation, powers of 10

From the Junk Drawer:

☐ Sidewalk chalk

☐ Accurate balance or scale that shows weight in grams

☐ Calculator

☐ Paper and pencil (or whiteboard and dry-erase marker; optional)

Step 1: Weigh a piece of sidewalk chalk. This must be done on a very accurate balance. You need a balance that will record the mass at least two places past the decimal point. The best at-home option will be a digital postal scale, if you have one. Fancy kitchen scales will do this, and almost all schools have balances that will do this. As a teacher, you may need to ask a science teacher to borrow one. One balance could handle an entire classroom if you allow the students to go a few at a time, but more balances would be quicker.

Step 2: Go outside and write your name (or a colorful design) on the sidewalk.

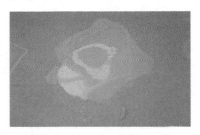

Step 3: Weigh the chalk when you come in. Subtract the final weight from the original weight. The "lost" weight is the chalk you left outside.

Step 4: To convert the lost weight to the number of molecules of chalk, you will have to use a little chemistry. Chalk is made of calcium carbonate ($CaCO^3$), which has molar mass of 100.09 grams. That means 100.09 grams of chalk has 6.02×10^{23} molecules of chalk. (The concept of a mole—6.02×10^{23}—is a topic you will learn in chemistry.)

The picture shows you how to do the calculation for the number of molecules of chalk on your sidewalk. You might need help putting the number in your calculator (or look at the explanation below). For fun and to show the usefulness of scientific notation, write out your answer in normal notation. That is done by moving the decimal point the same number as the power of 10. Put in 0s to hold the place for any values that aren't an integer.

$$\text{lost grams of chalk} \times \left(\frac{6.02 \times 10^{23} \text{ molecules}}{100.9 \text{ g } CaCO_3} \right)$$

The Math Behind It

Scientific notation uses powers of 10 to write very large and very small numbers, primarily in science. Ten to the second power (10^2) is 10×10 or 100. Ten to the fourth power (10^4) is $10 \times 10 \times 10 \times 10$ or 10,000. Writing 1.5×10^3 is the same as writing $1.5 \times 1,000$, or 1,500. The decimal place is moved three places to the right, because it was 10 to the third power. So 6.02×10^{23} (Avogadro's number) would be written as 602,000,000,000,000,000,000,000! This number is too big to fit in a calculator's display window in regular form, so scientific notation is useful.

Scientific calculators have a button labeled "EE" or "EXP." Pressing the button will show an E or a 10^x in your display. Type in the number before the multiplication sign, hit the EE (or EXP) key, then hit the powers above the 10 and your calculator can now handle it.

Scientists deal with extremely large numbers, like the diameter of the sun or the number of molecules in a sample, and extremely small numbers, like the diameter of an individual atom. Scientific notation is a valuable tool that helps integrate math into science.

Math for the Ages

This is a great cross-curricular activity for chemistry and algebra, but it is very doable even for students who haven't had chemistry yet. For high school students, the concept of a mole and Avogadro's number are probably familiar already. This is also great practice for using scientific notation on a calculator. High school teachers may want to talk to the chemistry teachers to see if they already do the lab. The teachers most likely will be flattered, and they may have a lab write-up already done.

Walking to Learn Slope

Use a stopwatch and a measuring tape to learn about the importance of slope. This activity is done with two people, one to record data and one to walk.

Algebra Concept: Slope

From the Junk Drawer:

- ☐ Outdoor area (or a very long hallway)
- ☐ Sidewalk chalk
- ☐ Measuring tape
- ☐ Helper
- ☐ Smartphone with stopwatch app (or stopwatch)
- ☐ Clipboard
- ☐ Paper and pencil
- ☐ Different-colored markers or pencils

Step 1: Draw a starting line on the sidewalk with chalk. Use a measuring tape and mark the following distances away from the starting point: 10 feet, 20 feet, 30 feet, 40 feet, 50 feet, and 60 feet. Use chalk to mark and label each of these distances. (If you're indoors, mark the ground with tape or sticky notes instead.)

Step 2: One helper will be the walker and one will be the timer and recorder. (If you have two helpers, you each can do a different task.) Set the smartphone stopwatch to 0. The walker will be moving at a slow, constant speed toward the 60-foot mark. The timer should also have a clipboard and paper to record the walker's times at each distance. The recorder should walk with the walker.

Step 3: Start the stopwatch as the walker starts walking. The recorder should write down the time for each distance up to the 60-foot mark.

distance (ft.)	time (s)		
0	0		
10	5.10		
20	10.29		
30	15.50		
40	20.75		
50	25.90		
60	31.02		

Step 4: Now repeat the activity and this time walk faster, but make sure to walk at a constant speed.

distance (ft.)	time (s)	time (s)	time (s)
0	0	0	0
10	5.10	3.30	2.80
20	10.29	6.75	5.70
30	15.50	10.05	8.89
40	20.75	13.25	11.62
50	25.90	16.51	14.32
60	31.02	19.74	17.05

Step 5: Plot the two sets of data on a graph. Put time on the *x*-axis and distance on the *y*-axis. Use a different color for each line. The slope of each line equals the average speed of the walker for each case.

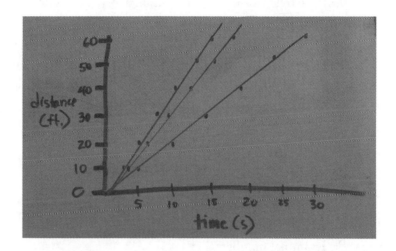

Step 6 (for classroom): This activity is great in the classroom environment. Place a different student with a stopwatch every 10 feet up to 60 feet. Three more students move as instructed, keeping a constant speed the entire distance. One will walk, one will walk faster, and one can jog (or walk very fast), one walker at a time. A starter will drop his or her arms and all timers will start their watches. Timers should stop their watches as the walker comes by and then record the data.

After all three walkers have participated, compile the timers' data on a whiteboard. Graph the data as described earlier.

The Math Behind It

The slope of a graph has meaning in the real world. Slope is defined as the change in the *y* variable divided by the change in the *x* variable. The easy way to remember this is "rise over run." The *y* variable for our graph was distance, and the *x* variable was time. So the slope is distance over time. Distance over time is the average speed of each walker in feet per second. In the classroom example, the slow walker would have the lowest value for the slope. The jogger would have the greatest slope.

Math for the Ages

This is a great hands-on way to teach the usefulness of slope. This is also a great cross-curricular activity for middle school, since often the same teacher teaches science and math. Almost all ages are capable of doing this lab once they have learned graphing.

This activity also can be used to teach the line of best fit. If the walkers kept a constant speed, the line should be straight. But since many people are using stopwatches, there will be some errors. The line of best fit averages out these errors.

Wheel of Theodorus

Create a piece of art and learn **irrational numbers** at the same time.

Algebra Concept: Irrational numbers

From the Junk Drawer:

☐ Paper

☐ Pencil

☐ Protractor

☐ Ruler

☐ Calculator (optional)

☐ Colored pencils or markers

Step 1: Draw two 1-inch-long lines on a piece of paper that are exactly 90 degrees apart.

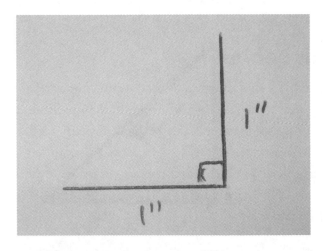

Step 2: Use a ruler to connect the two ends of the lines. This line would represent the hypotenuse of a right triangle. Using the Pythagorean theorem, you can solve that the length of the hypotenuse is equal to the square root of 2. This number is called an irrational number, which is a number that is not equal to the **ratio** of two integers.

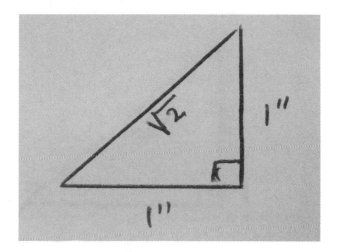

Step 3: Use the hypotenuse of that first triangle as the base of your next triangle. Use the protractor to draw another 1-inch line that is perpendicular to the hypotenuse of the previous triangle. Then draw in the new hypotenuse. The length of that hypotenuse is equal to the square root of 3.

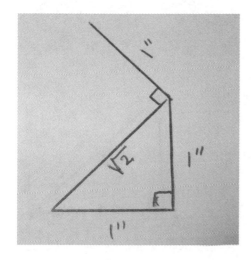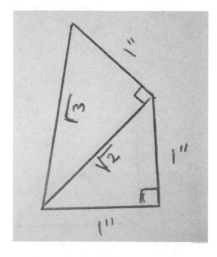

Step 4: Repeat Step 3 for a third triangle. The length of the hypotenuse is now the square root of 4 (which is equal to 2). Of course, 2 is *not* an irrational number.

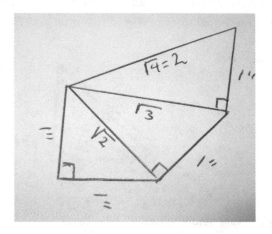

Step 5: Keep repeating until you have at least 15 triangles. As you add each triangle, write the length of the hypotenuse next to the line. Also, draw a small box in the corner to represent that the angle is 90 degrees.

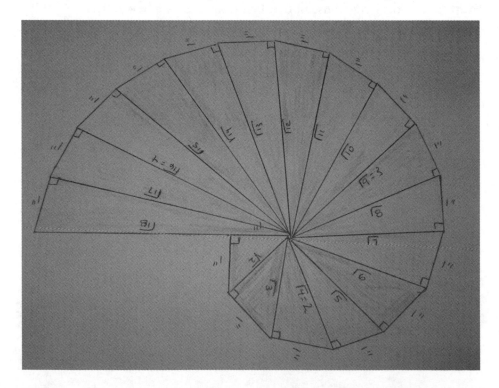

Step 6: You can also use the Wheel of Theodorus as part of a piece of artwork. Color each triangle differently—have fun and be creative.

The Math Behind It

Rational numbers are numbers that can be represented by a simple ratio of two numbers. The number 1.5 is a rational number because it can be represented by the ratio of 3 divided by 2. Rational numbers also end or repeat when dividing using a calculator. For example, 3 divided by 2 is equal to 1.5 exactly. And ⅓ is a rational number because it is equal to 0.3333—the 3s keep repeating forever.

Irrational numbers, however, will never repeat . . . ever. A calculator will show enough digits to fill up the display screen, but the number goes on forever. Pi is the most famous irrational number; it goes on forever. You probably use 3.14 in calculations, but pi has an infinite number of digits after that. Most of the square roots on your wheel are irrational numbers. The exceptions are the perfect squares: 4, 9, 16, and so on. They are rational numbers.

Theodorus was a math teacher for the famous Greek philosopher Plato. Plato wrote extensively and is considered one of the greatest minds ever. Most of what we know about Theodorus is found in the writings of Plato. The Wheel (or Spiral) of Theodorus and the concept of irrational numbers were his greatest contributions to math.

Math for the Ages

This activity is suitable for elementary-age students and up. Younger children could do it for fun but may struggle to make the measurements and make a perfect right angle. Middle school and high school students can easily do this activity and will enjoy the art side of the Wheel of Theodorus.

Wooden Graphs

Graph mass versus density for wood blocks to calculate a useful slope.

Algebra Concept: Slope

From the Junk Drawer:

☐ 5 different-sized wooden blocks (all the same type of wood)

☐ Ruler

☐ Paper and pencil

☐ Scale

☐ Computer or smartphone (optional)

☐ Graph paper

Step 1: Measure the length, width, and height of each wooden block in centimeters. Record the dimensions in a data chart. Then calculate the volume of each block by using length × width × height. The unit on your volumes will be centimeters cubed.

Step 2: Weigh each block on a scale. Kitchen scales will work in a home setting. If the scale is not calibrated in grams, use a computer or smartphone to convert the weight to mass in grams. In a classroom, teachers may already have balances that measure directly in grams. Some kitchen scales will also allow you to measure grams directly.

Step 3: For each block, graph mass on the y-axis against volume on the x-axis. Put all five points on the graph.

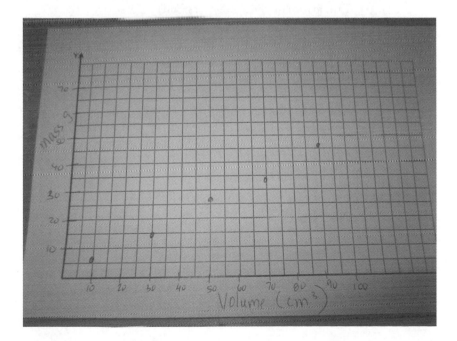

Step 4: Use a ruler to draw a straight line that indicates the direction of the points. This is the line of best fit.

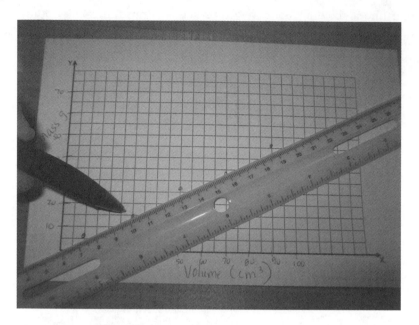

Step 5: Draw a triangle using the line as your hypotenuse. Label the height of the triangle (the *y* dimension, in grams) as the rise and base of the triangle (the *x* dimension, in centimeters cubed) as the run.

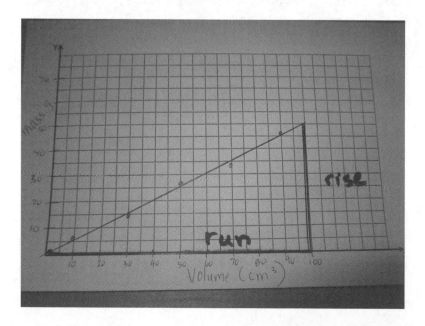

Step 6: Slope is equal to rise divided by run. Leave the units in the equation and the units on your answer will be grams divided by centimeters cubed. The slope will be equal to the density of the wood type.

The Math Behind It

This a great way to tie science and math together. The slope of a line tells you how steep the line is. Slope is a very common calculation in algebra. But it also is a very common calculation in science classes.

In this activity, the slope is the density of the wood. The number will be less than 1 gram per centimeter cubed. The density of water is 1.0 grams per centimeter cubed. Anything with a density *less than* 1, such as pine wood, will float on water. If the density is greater than 1 gram per centimeter cubed, the object will sink. Denser wood types, like oak, will have a greater density than pine. There are a few types of wood that sink in water. One is even called ironwood for that reason.

Math for the Ages

This activity is appropriate for almost any age, although younger students will need help with the measurements and calculations. You will probably need to find a woodworker to cut the small blocks. Many woodworkers also keep scraps and are more than willing to cut them for you. Older students might be able to use a handsaw to cut their own blocks. Try to use the same type of wood for the blocks so they have the same density. Pine is best and easiest to find. You could also use different types of wood to discuss why the points might not be in a straight line.

For teachers, if you cut 10 to 12 blocks, you can number them and use them for years. This is a great first-day-of-school lab if you have long class periods.

Yardstick Math

Cut an old yardstick to learn more about graphing.

Algebra Concepts: Graphing, slope, **extrapolation**

Adult supervision required

From the Junk Drawer:

☐ Saw

☐ 2 yardsticks (or meter sticks)

☐ Graph paper and pencil

☐ Ruler

☐ Postal scale (or accurate kitchen scale)

Step 1: With adult help (or permission), use a saw to cut a yardstick into several different lengths.

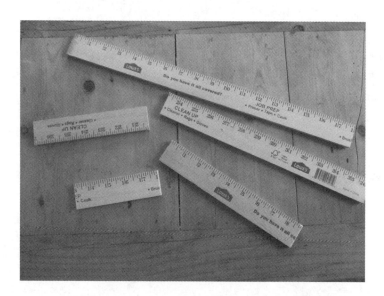

Step 2: On a piece of graph paper, create a set of axes. On the horizontal axis, number from 0 to beyond 36 if you are using a yardstick, adjusting for scale. For the graph shown below, each line is equal to 4 inches. Choose a

different scale if you are using a meter stick—perhaps each line is equal to 5 centimeters—since you will need to get beyond 100 centimeters.

On the vertical axis, number the ounces (or grams) based on what units you will use to measure weight. Most yardsticks are less than 8 ounces in weight, so as long as you have eight lines or more, you will be fine.

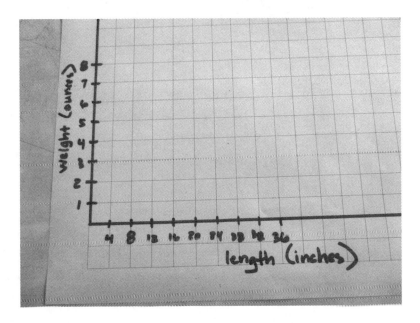

Step 3: Measure a single length of the cut yardstick with a ruler. Even though it has inches marked on it, measure the yardstick anyway since the saw removed some wood.

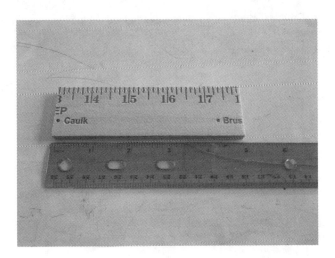

Step 4: Now, weigh the piece you just measured on the scale. Postal scales work really well, but accurate kitchen scales will also work. Plot the intersection of the piece's length and weight on the graph. Now, repeat Steps 3 and 4 for at least five pieces of the yardstick and graph the values.

Step 5: The points should lie in a pretty straight line. Use a ruler to draw the line of best fit. A line of best fit will average out any small errors in your measurements. You do not have to hit every point. The line of best fit does a better job of representing the actual measurements if there are as many points below the line as points above the line.

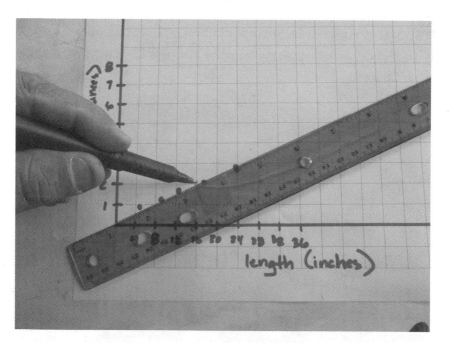

Step 6: Lay a ruler vertically on the line that represents 36 inches. Draw a light line up until it hits the angled line from the yardstick.

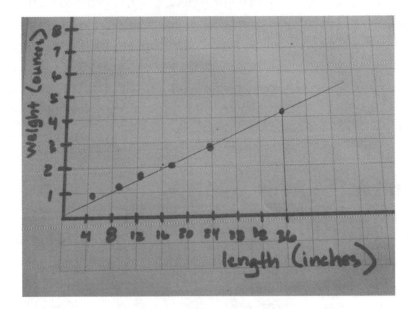

Step 7: From that point, lay the ruler horizontally and see what the whole yardstick weighs. If you have a separate uncut yardstick, one that is similar to the one you cut up, you can weigh it and compare. In a classroom setting, students can compare their values to those of other groups.

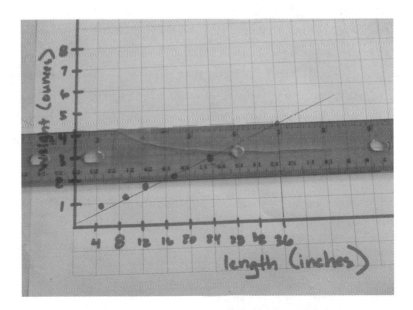

The Math Behind It

Graphing straight lines is important in algebra. Slope is a cool concept, but it is also useful. Once a line is created, it can be used to find useful data. If you read between the data points, it is called **interpolation**. If you extend a data line and read beyond the data points (as you did in this lab), it is called extrapolation. Of course, extrapolation assumes that the data line continues on, straight. Often that is a safe assumption, but be careful how far you continue the line.

Math for the Ages

This activity is appropriate for upper elementary and above. Most students will need help with the saw and cutting up the yardsticks. This may be a great way to involve parents or grandparents, to help with cutting. This is also another opportunity to discuss the line of best fit. This activity is also perfect with meter sticks, although they are harder to find (and more expensive) in the United States.

For a classroom, inexpensive yardsticks can be bought at home improvement stores, usually for under a dollar each. Cut them into lengths that can't be added up to 36 inches. This is also a way to use the yardsticks that accidentally get broken over the years. Once you finish this activity, wrap the pieces together with a rubber band and use them every year. Also, in a school setting, the science teachers will have accurate balances to weigh the pieces. If the sticks are made from different materials, they will not provide good results. But the students will be able to see why their results don't agree.

For upper level high school students, you can even add more layers. In my classroom, this activity is used to study error propagation. The students draw two lines of best fit. A line that represents the steepest slope possible from the data points and another line to represent the shallowest line of best fit. The actual weight of the yardstick should lie between those two lines.

Your Favorite Pi

Calculate pi using very simple tools.

Algebra Concepts: Graphing, pi

From the Junk Drawer:

☐ Paper and pencil

☐ 5–8 round objects (jar lids, bottles, balls, soup cans, etc.)

☐ Ruler (metric rulers make it easier to do decimals)

☐ Book

☐ String

☐ Graph paper

☐ Calculator (optional)

Step 1: Create a table with three columns. The first column is to record the name of the object you are measuring. The next column should be labeled *Diameter*. And the final column should be labeled *Circumference*.

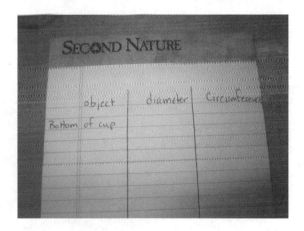

Step 2: Measure the diameter of your first object. The diameter is the widest distance across the round object (like jar lids and soup cans). Cups are great for this, since you have round but flat tops and bottoms. For spherical objects, keep reading on how to get the diameter, otherwise skip ahead to Step 3.

For spherical objects (like balls), place the object on a table and hold a book level, resting on top. Use a ruler to measure the distance from the tabletop to the bottom of the book, as shown. (You may have to account for the small gap at the end of the ruler, before the *0* line.)

Step 3: Wrap a string around the circumference (outside edge) of the round object. Pinch the string where it meets the starting end.

Step 4: Use a ruler to measure the length of the string. Record the measurement under *Circumference* in your table.

Step 5: On your graph paper, label the vertical *y*-axis *Circumference* and put the units you measured with in parentheses. Label the horizontal *x*-axis *Diameter* and put the units in parentheses.

Now decide how much each line on your graph paper will be equal to, called the graph's *scale*. To do this, find the largest circumference value. Put zero at the bottom of the vertical axis as shown. Your vertical axis must reach a number greater than the largest circumference you measured. Use convenient values for your scale. Each line should be a convenient and easy-to-use value, such as 2 each, 5 each, or 10 each. Label the lines going up the side. It is not necessary to label every line, but you should be able to decide the value for each line.

Label the horizontal axis using the same method.

Now it is time to plot your points.

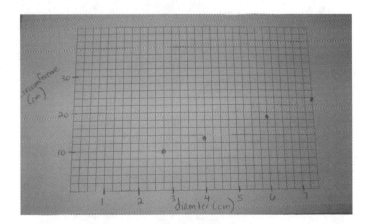

Step 6: The points should be in a straight line, but it is possible (and likely) that your points won't be perfectly straight. A good rule for straight lines is if your pencil can cover all the points, it is a straight line.

Use a ruler to draw the best straight line that shows the general direction of the data. It is OK not to hit every point. The line should average out the high and low points. In math, they call this a line of best fit.

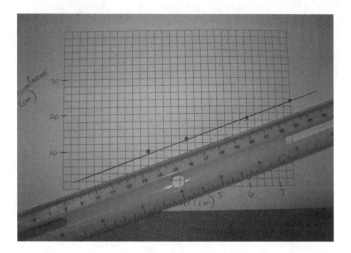

Step 7: You want to calculate the slope of this line. In math, slope tells you how steep the line is, and the number often means something important. The easy way to remember slope is that the slope is equal to "rise over run." That means how much the line rises (vertical distance, or *y*) divided by how much it runs (horizontal distance, or *x*).

Draw a triangle directly on your graph paper. The angled line is what you are going to use as the third side of your triangle. Draw the triangle large to make your task easier. Also, it is smart to use convenient lines for the two non-angled sides. Slope is equal to rise divided by run. Is the value you got close to a familiar number?

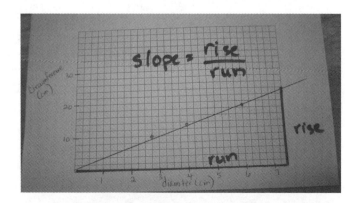

The Math Behind It

Circumference is equal to π × diameter. The equation has been known for centuries, but it is still true today. Graphs tells us mathematical relationships. Circumference versus diameter is what math and science people call a **direct relationship**. That means when one value doubles, the other value doubles. When one value triples, the other one triples, and so on.

The slope of a graph will also often tell you something. In this case, the slope is the constant discovered in about 2500 BC. The Greeks and the Babylonians both had a pretty good estimate of the value of pi by 1900 BC. The true value of pi is quite amazing in the fact that it goes on forever without a pattern. Most of us learned pi's value as 3.14, but in reality it is 3.14159265 . . . and on forever.

Graphs also allow math and science people to create equations. The basic equation for a straight line is $y = m \times x + b$. The last letter, b, is called the y-intercept. This is the point where the line intersects the y-axis. In our graph, the y-intercept is 0, since the line goes through the origin. So the equation for this graph is $y = mx$. The y-axis is circumference (C) and the x-axis is diameter (d), so the equation becomes $C = m \times d$. The slope is m, and for circles, the slope is pi. So this equation is $C = (\pi) \times d$. Since the diameter is two times the radius (r), the equation is sometimes written as $C = 2 (\pi) \times r$.

Math for the Ages

For preschoolers, pi might be a difficult concept. Just teaching diameter, radius, and circumference is probably enough.

For younger elementary students, this is a great activity to teach them the basics of graphing and measuring. You might have to guide them some as they work, and they will need detailed instructions, like those provided above.

For upper elementary and middle school students, this activity is easy enough for them to grasp and gives them a great introduction to the meaning of slope. Most have probably been exposed to pi by this point and should recognize that is what the slope is. Depending on their level, they may not need as much instruction.

For high school students, this activity is a must. In my physics classes, this is my day one activity. It helps me as a teacher see if my students understand how to graph and calculate slope. They get virtually no instructions, so it serves as an inquiry-based activity. This lets me know if I need to teach graphing to these students.

Many math teachers (and some science teachers) make a big day of Pi Day (3/14). Now you have a new holiday to celebrate and a reason to eat pie.

Memorizing Pi

Have you ever heard the saying, "How I wish I could calculate pi"? The number of letters in each word is equal to the digits in pi, so it is 3.141592.

How I wish I could calculate pi?
3 . 1 4 1 5 9 2

Pi is an irrational number that never repeats and has an infinite number of digits after the decimal point. The number 3.14 is commonly used, but as problems become more complex, more precision is needed. The saying "How I wish I could calculate pi" is a mnemonic, a short and easy way to help remember something. Pi is introduced at a young age and shows up again in geometry but is very useful in some algebra functions.

Glossary

area: The measurement of a surface.

bar graph(s): A graph containing upright blocks (bars) to show values.

box plot: A graphical way to show the spread of measured values.

commutative property: A mathematical property that states that multiplication can be performed in any order.

coordinates: Parts of an ordered pair that locate a point on a graph, usually expressed as (x,y). The x value and the y value are coordinates.

direct relationship: A mathematical function where both quantities change by the same amount.

distributive property: A mathematical property that states that a number multiplied by the sum of two numbers is the same as multiplying each value by the first number and adding them. For example, $2 \times (4 + 5)$ is the same as $2 \times 4 + 2 \times 5$. Both are equal to 18.

equation: An expression in math using an equal sign.

exponential decay function(s): A mathematical function that shows a value decreasing by a consistent percentage over a period of time.

extrapolation: Reading a value off a graph that is outside of the measured values.

factor: An integer (counting number) that divides equally into a larger integer.

factorial(s): The product of all the integers below and including the number, expressed as $n!$. For example, $3! = 3 \times 2 \times 1$.

FOIL: An acronym for first, outside, inside, last. Used to help multiply polynomials.

hypotenuse: The longest side of a right triangle.

inequality: An equation that uses < or > instead of an equal sign.

integer: A counting number.

interpolation: Reading values off a graph between the measured values.

inverse function: A function in which one value goes down as the other value goes up.

irrational number: A number in decimal form that never ends. Pi is the most famous irrational number.

line of best fit: A line on a graph that shows the best approximation of the average points.

mean: The average of a group of numbers.

median: The middle of a group of numbers.

mode: The number that occurs most often in a group of numbers.

ordered pair(s): A pair of coordinates, usually in parentheses as (x,y), used to locate a point on a graph.

parabola(s): A mathematical function in which one value is directly related the square of the other value, such as $y = x^2$.

perfect square(s): A number that has two factors that are exactly the same. For example, 9 is a perfect square because it is 3×3.

pi: An irrational number that relates circumference to the diameter of a circle, indicated with the symbol π. Its value is 3.1415926 . . .

pie graph(s): A circular graph where the size of each wedge represents a percent of 100.

polynomial(s): An expression of multiple terms, involving a mathematical operation. For example, $3x + 4$ is a polynomial.

powers of 10: Ten raised to an integer value. For example, $10^3 = 10 \times 10 \times 10 = 1,000$. Useful to describe very small and large numbers in scientific notation.

pressure: Force per unit area.

probability: The likelihood that something will happen.

Pythagorean theorem: An equation used to solve for one side of a right triangle, $a^2 + b^2 = c^2$.

radical(s): Any expression that contains the square root symbol ($\sqrt{}$).

range: Two numbers defining the lowest to the highest values in a group.

ratio: A comparison of two numbers. For example, if you have three apples and two are yellow, the ratio of yellow apples to total apples is 2/3, which can also be written as 2:3.

rational number(s): Any number that can be represented as a ratio of integers.

scientific notation: A shorthand way to express extremely large and small numbers.

slope(s): How steep a line is on a graph, calculated as rise/run.

square root(s): A number that, when multiplied by itself, gives you the original number. For example, 2 is the square root of 4, or $2 = \sqrt{4}$.

transitive property: A mathematical property that states if $a = b$ and $b = c$, then $a = c$.

x-axis: The horizontal axis on a graph.

y-axis: The vertical axis on a graph.

Also available from Chicago Review Press

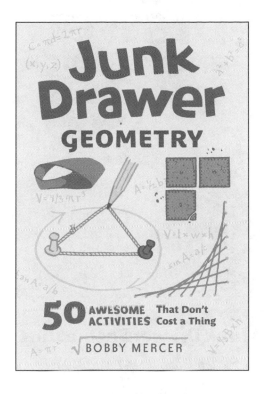

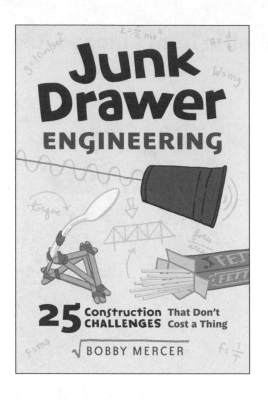

Junk Drawer Engineering

50 Construction Challenges That Don't Cost a Thing

by Bobby Mercer

420 B/W Photos

"The compilation and suggested modifications for youngsters with different backgrounds and skill sets make this particularly welcome for science teachers as well as young learners. . . . Hours of fun for STEM-inclined kids, parents, caregivers, and teachers." — *Kirkus Reviews*

Trade Paper • 224 pages • ISBN: 978-1-61373-716-3

$14.99 (CAN $19.99) • Ages 9 and up

Junk Drawer Chemistry

50 Awesome Experiments That Don't Cost a Thing

by Bobby Mercer

230 B/W Photos

"Very highly recommended for family, school, and community library instructional reference collections." —*Midwest Book Review*

Trade Paper • 224 pages • ISBN: 978-1-61373-179-6

$14.95 (CAN $17.95) • Ages 9 and up

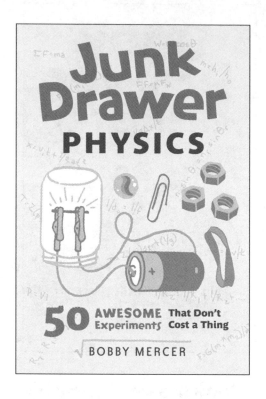

Junk Drawer Physics

50 Awesome Experiments That Don't Cost a Thing

by Bobby Mercer

230 B/W Photos

"More than enough to keep scientifically curious kids busy on rainy days."
—*Publishers Weekly*

Trade Paper • 208 pages • ISBN: 978-1-61374-920-3

$14.95 (CAN $17.95) • Ages 9 and up